A DO
ADOR

AÚ

MARACANÁ

SÃO
CRISTÓVÃ

BAÍA
DE
GUANABARA

TIJUCA

MANGUEIRA

GAMBOA

CENTRO

COVADO

LAR

BOTAFO

PORTO
OS
ONT

BANA

ATLÂNTICO

Rio de Janeiro

Bossa Nova:
The Story of the Brazilian Music that Seduced the World

Garrincha:
The Triumph and Tragedy of Brazil's Forgotten
Footballing Hero

Rio de Janeiro

Carnival under Fire

Ruy Castro

Translated by John Gledson

BLOOMSBURY

Published by Bloomsbury, New York and London
Distributed to the trade by Holtzbrinck Publishers

All papers used by Bloomsbury are natural, recyclable products made
from wood grown in well-managed forests. The manufacturing processes
conform to the environmental regulations of the country of origin.

Library of Congress Cataloging-in-Publication Data

Castro, Ruy, 1948-
[Carnaval no fogo. English]
Rio de Janeiro : carnival under fire / Ruy Castro; translator, John Gledson.
  p. cm. -- (Writer and the city)
ISBN 1-58234-190-7 (hardcover)
1. Rio de Janeiro (Brazil)--Description and travel. 2. Rio de Janeiro
(Brazil)--Social life and customs. 3. Rio de Janeiro (Brazil)--History.
I. Title. II. Series.

F2646.C3713 2004
918.1'530465--dc22
                    2004000159

First U.S. Edition 2004

1 3 5 7 9 10 8 6 4 2

Typeset by Hewer Text Ltd, Edinburgh
Printed in Great Britain by Clays Ltd, St Ives plc

To the Ruas Paissandu and Barão do Flamengo

PROLOGUE

In the last week of February 2003, gangsters linked to the drug traffic unleashed a wave of violence in Rio. They set fire to buses in the city's outskirts, had shoot-outs with the police in the favelas, and set off cinema-type car chases on the motorways. The city became apprehensive. Carnival was round the corner, and Rio was expecting hundreds of thousands of tourists. The hotels had a record number of bookings, the weather forecast predicted five days of sunshine hot enough to melt a cathedral, and the cariocas had already sold their souls to Brahma – a beer brand, not a god. In the vital process of working themselves up for the big show, Carnival groups were already on the streets, though according to the calendar the holiday hadn't yet begun.

On the Monday before Carnival, in a reprisal for the toughening of their boss's prison conditions, young louts on motorcycles tried to force shopkeepers in some neighbourhoods to shut their premises. Five months earlier, in September 2002, they'd already successfully done this. But this time, the city adopted Hemingway's motto when threatened by elephants: 'elegance under pressure'. Not all the shopkeepers obeyed orders. And there were other, very carioca forms of resistance.

In Ipanema, just as two gangsters, somewhat more daring than the others, were trying to make a supermarket pull down its doors, the samba group *Vem Ni Mim Que Sou Facinha* [Harass Me, I'm Willing] was getting ready to start up in its home base fifteen yards away, the little nameless square in front of the Zig-Zag bar, near the Praça General Osório. The Facinha wasn't going to let anything get in the way of its Carnival. One of the participants was stretching out a banner calling people together; another was checking the sound equipment; a third was organising the sale of T-shirts with the group's logo on them; yet another had charge of a crucial part of the operation – jamming cans of beer into enormous ice-filled poly-styrene containers. When everything was ready, the beautiful, black, stout seventy-year-old Tereza, the Facinha's flag-bearer, gave two steps forward with her banner. The tambourines rattled, and hundreds of people launched into the samba written for that year by the group's composers. When they heard the song, with words all about happiness and good vibes, it may have been that, for many of the tradesmen on the block, life had returned to normal – and, while at other times they might have given in to the gangsters' pressure, they changed their minds and opened their doors. The club leapt and danced all night. Carnival, as always, had re-established the moral balance.

It was perfect. In the five days of Carnival proper, around 200 groups and bands paraded through Rio's streets, with more than a million people in their wake. In the Sambodrome, the samba schools put on a show of an extravagance and euphoria not seen for many years. In every area of the city, even those where conflict was a way of life, the dances in the open squares kept masses of people going till dawn. The city nearly drowned in *feijoada* (the traditional dish of black bean stew) – there'd never been so much, in the restaurants or the hotels. The happiness and high jinks drowned out the headlines speaking of violence and fear. The presence of the army ensured that every carioca had the right to his or her Carnival.

In those few days, Rio welcomed 400,000 tourists – who, when they were asked by the research institutes about the violence question, said they'd seen nothing out of the ordinary. Spread around the processions, dances, parties and junketings, they had a great time, took their clothes off like the natives, kissed each other in their millions, made love, laughed and fell head over heels for each other; at last they understood what Carnival in Rio *was*. Long after Ash Wednesday, most of them were still around. They'd never seen anything like it.

Even for the cariocas, who for centuries have been putting this spectacle on and starring in it,

Carnival 2003 was one for the record books. It was Carnival under fire – but there was nothing new about that. That's the way Rio has lived during the centuries of its history – and not just in February.

CHAPTER ONE

Two or three Decembers ago, Marize Araújo, a Brazilian advertising executive living in Lisbon, came to spend the Christmas and new year holidays in Rio. A mutual friend of ours, the architect Ana Luiza Pinheiro, went to pick her up at Galeão airport. Marize is carioca and she held an unusual record for carioca expatriates: she hadn't been back to the city for three years. It was a daytime flight, but it was dark by the time the plane had landed. Half an hour later, happily chattering away to Ana Luiza on her way to Ipanema, she hadn't the least idea that in a short while, she would have the greatest reception of her life – the greatest that any carioca could have imagined.

The car came through the two halves of the Rebouças tunnel and, at the very moment when the vision of the Rodrigo de Freitas lagoon opened out in front of her, fireworks shot into the sky, bursting in coloured lights mirrored in the still water. Marize was shocked. That in itself would have been a terrific welcome, but if the display programmer had been the devil himself equipped with a battery of computers, the result couldn't have been more infernal. Along with the fireworks, layer upon layer of mini lights, two and a half million of them, lit up a huge Christmas tree, floating right in the middle of the lagoon. And, at the same time, the fanfares of a symphony orchestra playing '*Cidade maravilhosa*', Rio's euphoric anthem, came out of loudspeakers among the clouds. Almost breathless, tears gushing out, Marize asked Ana Luiza to stop the car – she wanted to see and hear the spectacle the city had prepared for her.

It was an accident, of course. Her arrival had merely coincided with the opening ceremony for the Christmas tree that, for some years now, a company has been setting afloat in the lagoon in early December. The fireworks and the orchestra playing '*Cidade maravilhosa*' are part of the proceedings. But, for Marize, how magical that this should happen just at that very moment.

For me, with its conjunction of coincidences, this story beats another – famous, though with a whiff of fiction about it – concerning an Irish sailor whose religious faith was about to drown in whisky, and who landed in Rio on the night of 12 October 1931. Stepping out on to Mauá Square, he glanced up into the night sky and up there, far away, Jesus Christ arose from nowhere: gleaming, upright, hovering, with his arms open over the city. When he saw this vision, the sailor almost had a heart attack. He thought the alcohol was making him see things. But it might be a sign, too, a warning that God wasn't going to let him lose his soul to a distillery. He ran back to the ship, shut himself in his quarters, swore never to drink again, and gave himself up to the chaplain – who, if he knew what had really happened, decided not to disappoint the sailor. How was the sailor going to believe that the Christ was a soapstone statue as high as a ten-storey building, planted on the crest of a rock 2,000 feet above sea level and whose illumination was just at that very moment being switched on for the first time? And that this lighting had nothing supernatural about it, except that it was being provided, from a distance, by Guglielmo Marconi, the inventor of radio? Marconi had sent out an electric signal from his ship *Electra*, anchored in the Bay of Naples, which in its turn had been picked up by a receiver in Dorchester, England, retransmitted to an antenna on the other side of the Atlantic, in Jacarepaguá in Rio, and then sent up to the statue on the top of the Corcovado – now that really was difficult to believe.

Coming in to Rio is so spectacular that throughout the centuries, for anyone arriving by plane or ship, it has set off these alterations in perception. It must have been the same in summer 1502, when a Portuguese fleet commanded by Gonçalo Coelho came into Guanabara bay for the first time. Its chief pilot, the Florentine Amerigo Vespucci, thought the bay was a river mouth. And, since it was 1 January, he called the place Rio de Janeiro – a name we all love, and immediately shorten to plain Rio. Still today historians ask how Vespucci, a pilot who had sailed the seven seas, and an ace in cosmography, managed to confuse a bay with a river. Well, maybe he was bowled over by the setting, and if that's the case, he wasn't the only one – just the first. Another theory is that in old Portuguese, 'rio' was just another word for a bay. In that case, Vespucci made no mistake. A quick look at his c.v. might persuade us not to underestimate him when it comes to naming things. For example; Columbus might have discovered America – but who invented the expression 'New World', and ended up giving his name to the new-found continent? The daring Amerigo Vespucci – the same man who baptised Rio.

If Vespucci returned to the city today, 500 years on, what would he think? In 1502, when he faced the Sugar Loaf, he saw in Guanabara something very like the idea the ancients had of Paradise: a riotous display of hills and mountain-ranges, beaches, inlets, islands, dunes, sandbanks, mangrove swamps, lagoons and forests, all this under an endless blue sky. A masterpiece of nature, inhabited by happy, sunburnt and amoral people: men and women who spent all their time singing and dancing in the sun, everybody naked, cheerfully fornicating in the woods and on the sand, sleeping in hammocks by moonlight or in romantic straw huts, and surrounded by an abundance of fruit, birds and fish, all within reach – you didn't have to plant, just pluck, as long as you lived. It was a life so idyllic, so like Paradise, that it left little room for the idea, then current among the Jesuits, that the savages didn't have a 'soul'.

In 2002, Vespucci would see both similarities and differences to this unbeatable collection of picture-postcard views. The bay would be as spectacular, only now, if he looked at it closely, he would find it fouled by foreign bodies such as plastic bottles, old tyres or 1,000 tons of oil emptied into the sea by a tanker. The outline of the coast would still be astonishing, but Vespucci, who knew it when it was virgin, would notice it had been altered – where had all the dozens of delightful inlets, tiny islands and beaches gone? The big mountains would still be there, firm as sentinels, though their green covering has receded a great deal. The temperature would have gone up a lot too, and he'd be dying to take off those tight velvet breeches and his Elizabethan jacket. But he wouldn't condemn every human intervention on the landscape – he would certainly love the cable car, hanging from its wires, going up and down the Sugar Loaf. And wherever he looked, he would find the explanation for all these trans-formations: instead of the village with its scattered huts, a city has arisen, with high, white buildings, inhabited by 5.8 million people called cariocas – almost all of them with souls.

Vespucci would also recognise some old customs. Many of the natives would still live half their lives on the beaches, practically naked. At a certain time of the year, they'd do nothing else but sing and dance to drum music, except they'd be covered with strange costumes, and seem to obey a kind of choreography. And the huts that now invaded the hills would no longer be built of straw, but wood and masonry. If he got off his ship and wandered through the streets, Vespucci would find himself in a city that is old and modern, welcoming and impersonal, restrained and permissive, civilised and barbarous – with contradictions that, maybe more than in other big cities, would make him feel as if he was in heaven and hell at the same time. And even for him, used as he was to the lairs of the most ferocious buccaneers, it would be enormously exciting.

To foreign eyes, during its 500 years of history, Rio has been, in succession: an Eden dreamt of by utopians; the failed Antarctic France; a port for pirates and corsairs; a market for gold and slaves; the capital of a European empire; a court out of an operetta; the Marvellous City; the land of Carnival; and always, even if on the quiet, a kind of sexual Mecca. It has also upheld the tradition of happily receiving and giving shelter to whoever had arrived here: soldiers, missionaries, victims of racial persecution, political refugees, religious rebels, immigrants from all over the place and even fugitives from justice. Ronald Biggs, the Great Train Robber, wasn't the first to ask himself: 'What if I ran away to Rio?' Long before him, in 1950, Alec Guinness had already had the same idea in Charles Crichton's film *The Lavender Hill Mob* – the difference is that Biggs did really come down here. Curiously, Brazilians who rob others' money, whether it be public or private, go in the other direction: they flee to Miami or Europe.

Rio welcomes everyone, and asks no questions. The city – a strip of land entrenched between chains of mountains and a coastline with nearly fifty miles of beach – is a permanent promise of sun, good humour and freedom of movement. And, except for an occasional rainstorm, a defeat for the Flamengo football team (which anyway cheers up half the city), or some other little local difficulty, it always fulfils its promises. Recently, in 2003, it was elected by the *New Scientist* as 'the friendliest city in the world'. Just for the record, the 'least friendly' was New York.

If you count the period between 1640 and 1763, when it shared the responsibility with Bahia, Rio was Brazil's capital for 320 years – until 1960, when Brasília was founded, a theme park given over to politics and wheeler-dealing. During all this time, Rio was also the country's official entrance-way and its main symbol. The mere sight of images like the Sugar Loaf, the pavements along Copacabana beach, Christ the Redeemer or the Maracanã stadium let the foreigner know what country this was. This didn't change when it ceased to be the capital: Rio is still the city by which people identify Brazil.

This has its good and bad sides. Geography is not one of humanity's favourite subjects, so that anything, for good or ill, that's going on in Brazil's 3.3 million square miles is thought of outside Brazil as happening here. A forest catches fire in Amazonia and it's thought someone in Rio has something to do with it – no one's obliged to know that Rio is further away from Manaus than Lisbon from Moscow. For the same reason, there are people who think cariocas have to grapple with alligators in broad daylight, or that snakes get into apartments and wrap themselves round the legs of little old ladies while they're doing their knitting. Of course such things don't happen, but it is comforting to know that it's true that, in some of the more hidden, seductive areas of the city – like the Horto, the Gávea, Urca and Cosme Velho, all of them near the forest and still full of houses with verandas and backyards – one can still see gangs of small monkeys swinging on the electric wiring or chatting with the locals a couple of feet away from their windows. These monkeys must be the great-great-great-grandchildren of the ones Charles Darwin caught when he came to Rio in 1832 with the *Beagle*, and from which sprung some revolutionary ideas about the origin of species. Rio is also frequently visited by sea-otters, dolphins and penguins, and the other day a pair of capybaras was seen swimming in the Rodrigo de Freitas lagoon, among the pedalos and sailing boats. The best visitor in recent times, however, was a five-foot-long turtle, weighing 660 pounds, which laid thirty-eight eggs on Macumba beach. Since we know that, wherever they migrate to, turtles come back to their native beach to lay, here we have, in the twenty-first century, a true carioca turtle, with a respect for tradition.

However much men have tried to destroy it over all those centuries of its existence, Rio has resisted the urbicide which has laid other cities waste. Of all the great modern cities, it's one of the few that can be easily recognised on seventeenth-century maps and engravings – there one can see the mountains that to this day form the carioca skyline. There's no lack of that kind of iconography, though many of the originals are in European museums and private collections. From its very early days, Rio has been visited by English, French and German painters, who felt the power of its natural setting, and were thrilled by the opportunity it gives to portray it from above, with the artist perched on top of a mountain. It wasn't just painters; later, photographers did this too. Rio was the first city in the world to be photographed from the air – in 1840, almost seventy years before Santos-Dumont invented flying. When they climbed mountains like the Corcovado or the Tijuca with their equipment on muleback, they were able to take their photos more than 2,000 feet up, higher than any of the pioneer planes were able to go. There are books and more books full of these photos.

It was this stockpile of memory that saved the

city. Though thousands of buildings from the colonial period have been knocked down, whole
neighbourhoods thrown into the sea and the edge
of the bay very much altered, the past is present in
every street. In Rio there are more baroque
churches than shopping malls, more museums than
motels, and incontestably more French fountains
and statues cast in the Val d'Osne than public
lavatories – in fact, after Paris, it's the city with
the most French statuary in the world.

But, since Rio is in Brazil, a country where the
rich are ridiculously rich, the poor frighteningly
poor, and the majority fall into the latter camp,
the city has always reflected this disparity. Even so,
at least until a short time ago, it was the city that
had best learnt to live with the problem. Here, over
the centuries, rich and poor have kept friction to a
minimum by frequenting the same spaces, like the
beaches, football stadiums, bars, samba schools,
and Carnival clubs – there's no one more democratic and less apartheid-minded than the carioca.

No one is more used to danger, either. In the
eighteenth century, as the historian Maria Fernanda
Bicalho has shown in her book *A cidade e o Império*
[The City and the Empire], Rio was already living
on high alert. At night, the streets were taken over
by men wrapped in cloaks, armed with knives and
daggers – footpads, assassins, tramps, beggars,
gypsies, slaves either on the run or practised in
the arts of *capoeira*, all of them with the worst
of intentions. It's hardly surprising that, even on a

moonlit night, social life in the colony was a fiasco. Smuggling was part of daily life, with ships being relieved of their cargo and bodies left to the mercy of the tides, all with the already efficient connivance of the police. And then there was the external menace; the gold that flowed out from Minas Gerais came through Rio, which turned the city into a consumer's dream for foreign pirates; invasion was a frequent possibility. It only actually happened twice, in 1710 and 1711, but even when the pirates didn't come, the rumour-mongers spread panic and then ransacked abandoned houses. Little by little, the carioca population incorporated these perils into their lifestyle, learning to recognise whether the danger was real or not. By the nineteenth and twentieth centuries, they had achieved a savvy enviable even by the standards of much more violent cities like Chicago and New York.

Lately, this savvy has been put to the test by the same plague that's reached other places: drugs and the violence associated with them. The steep – at times almost vertical – hills (called *morros* in Portuguese), which provide the city's unique topography and have inspired thousands of sambas, have been occupied by drug-trafficking gangs and have become the setting for battles with the police, or between the gangs themselves, making life hell for the honest, poor people who live there. Each favela is a kasbah, only without the charm of Pépé le Moko's hideout – quite to the contrary, the local bandits have not an ounce of class. From time to time, one of them is promoted to being the big boss of organised crime, and the press dedicates headlines to his accomplishments (strangely enough, only in Rio are bandits famous). Once caught in the shack where he lives and duly put away, we discover that he is a guy without a shirt on his back, with a large belly overhanging his threadbare bermudas – a belly produced by the pizzas provided daily by suppliers outside the jail. Does anyone believe that someone like that can 'organise' crime? It's more likely that this role belongs to one or more brains of the Professor Moriarty or Dr Mabuse variety – men in blazers and scarves who control the flow and the laundering of money, the reception and distribution of drugs, the purchase of arms and the corruption of the legal system from their three-storey penthouses in the posh parts of town. In countries like the United States, these things are dealt with on a federal level. In Brazil, until a short while ago, each state had to look after itself.

Rio doesn't manufacture arms, doesn't refine cocaine and doesn't have even a single flowerpot in its gardens to grow marijuana. But it all flows in and out over its borders, generating fortunes used to polish and lubricate an arsenal worthy of an army, and to bribe policeman, lawyers, judges and politicians. When they're jailed, the foot-soldier traffickers are installed in 'maximum security' cells where they have mobile phones, the Internet, radio, cable TV, newspapers, magazines, a microwave, air-conditioning, champagne in the minibar, 'intimate' visits and legal assistance that would make large companies envious – in 2002, there was one case of a prisoner who was visited by seven different lawyers on the same day. With all this comfort and security, they manage to run their businesses from inside their cells, selling big allocations of drugs, monitoring operations from a distance, and allowing their jailers to trade their car in for a new one twice a year. It's even thought that, if there is such a thing as 'organised' crime, it's to be found inside the police force. Not that this is any protection – the Rio police kill and die at a rate comparable with the highest in the world.

Almost every day there is some violent scene, with car chases using the latest models, shoot-outs between the police and the drug-traffickers, an occasional burnt-out bus, and innocent people are caught in the crossfire. For anyone from outside who only knows Rio from television, it's as if no one here has any respite. However, that's not exactly the real situation. The greater part of the fighting takes place on the *morros* themselves or on the motorways into the city. Just as in the rest of the country, ninety-nine per cent of cariocas only find out about it on TV. In Rio, unfortunately, everything tends to be so visible for the rest of the country that any occurrence is magnified. 'I'm not afraid of the facts, only of headlines,' as the humorist Millôr Fernandes says.

And then there's the other side of the coin. While

the police go up one hillside and exchange fire with a gang of traffickers, perhaps, on the neighbouring hill poor children are being taught drama under UNESCO's auspices. Or an Italian photography team is doing a fashion special for Benetton. Or a caravan of jeeps full of tourists are enjoying themselves in the Rocinha favela. And, far from the *bangue-bangue* (as Brazilians say), the beaches are full of people whose major problem is attracting the attention of the person selling beer or ice-lollies. But that's not 'news'.

The city is far too grown-up to allow itself to be engulfed in fear, and cariocas are born with the genes to face it. At the same time as, in some street in the centre of the city, there's a running battle between street-salesmen and the police, there are people 200 yards away researching sixteenth-century documents in the National Library, or hunting out rare bossa nova LPs in the open-air market on the Rua Pedro Lessa. On 30 September 2002, the day the drug traffic exceeded itself in daring and tried to force the shops in Ipanema to shut, the carioca poet Apicius launched his exquisite book *A baleia* [The Whale] in a bookshop in that same neighbourhood. It was a splendid evening, with wine and canapés, and all his friends were there. 'Poetry's a form of resistance, don't you think?' he said to me excitedly.

Another poet, Ezra Pound, who went through much worse experiences, once asked, apropos of Venice: 'What do we have to pay for so much beauty?' In Rio, the payment is in a hard currency: excitement. It's one of the world's most exciting cities – perhaps a bit too exciting. It has to be – just because we don't have access to certain calamities that punctuate daily life in more peaceful cities. Here we're safe from volcanoes, earthquakes, avalanches, hurricanes, tornados, electric storms, seaquakes, tsunamis, geological faults and blizzards. It is true that this last possibility, sudden blizzards, can't be ruled out – many of the outdoor clocks, which give the temperature as well as the time, put a + next to the figure in centigrade. So, one glorious sunny afternoon in Copacabana, we are told that the temperature is +33°C. Which is comforting to know, when we're sweating on the beach – and if the sub-zero temperatures the clocks seem to envisage actually materialise, we'll all be caught in our swimming-trunks or bikinis.

Also, Rio has no suicide-bombers, radical separatists, young neo-Nazis who beat up immigrants, sexual perverts, men who strangle rich old women, spotty youths who shoot their schoolmates dead, psychopathic snipers and other dangerous maniacs who contribute to the fame of Scotland Yard and the FBI. If it's any consolation, there aren't many madmen here – only gangsters. Daily life, incredible as it might seem, can be so uneventful that, the other day, the mother of a friend of mine excused herself, saying she had an appointment with her 'serial killer'. We all got a shock, till it turned out she'd made a mistake – she'd meant to say 'personal trainer'!

But it remains true that, for a city where every-thing should encourage leisure and relaxation – men and women flat on their backs, sipping coconut-milk, fanned by cool sea breezes and whistling 'The Girl from Ipanema' – Rio does have too much electricity. This isn't something that came about today, or yesterday. It's been there from the beginning.

Our Indians, for example, had been here for more than 1,000 years, quiet as mice, happily killing and eating one another, when they saw the silhouette of a sail on the horizon – Vespucci's, in 1502. And that was it. Their lives were changed for ever. And the lives of their 'discoverers' too, as we'll see.

There is a thesis that it was the Guanabara Indians, the Tupinambás, who inspired *In Praise of Folly* by Erasmus of Rotterdam (1508), Sir Thomas More's *Utopia* (1516), one of Montaigne's *Essays* (the famous 'On the Cannibals' of 1580), the treatises on Natural Law by German and Dutch jurists in the seventeenth century, and, on into the eighteenth, the works of thinkers like Montesquieu, Diderot and Voltaire, till we come to Rousseau's 'noble savage' and from there to the motto of the French Revolution itself: 'Liberty, Equality, Fraternity'. Strange, but true.

The idea that our own dear Tupinambás should have set off such a political and philosophical riot in

Europe seems absurd even to us cariocas; we're more used to seeing them represented each year by the members of a traditional Carnival *bloco*, the Cacique de Ramos. But the thesis makes sense when we trace the genealogy of these books: they all start from a famous letter sent by Amerigo Vespucci to the banker Lorenzo de' Medici in 1502 and which was read throughout Europe in the ensuing decades. No tourist agency would ever produce anything to match it – for Vespucci was almost selling tickets to heaven.

The idea of a kind of earthly branch of the biblical Eden, where no one would need written laws to be happy for evermore, existed long before 1500. The problem was that no one knew where this Eden was, or what the visiting times were. But with the great voyages came the discoveries and the first contact with the peoples of tropical lands. Finally, here was an Eden on show, even better than the one in Genesis – and, from what Vespucci said, it was in Rio. Why?

Because, here, amid the most exuberant natural setting one could imagine, there lived a sweet, innocent people, with no notions of government, money, material goods or private property, without greed, envy or selfishness, and remote from any idea of good or evil. Without sin, too, for in Guanabara's everlasting summer, men, women, children, and old people went around naked day and night, without a single eyebrow being raised. And, contrary to what one might think, they weren't wild beasts with their bodies covered in hair or a third eye in their forehead, but a pleasant, sociable people of great physical beauty and enough health to make any European envious. 'Natural man', the direct descendant of Adam, really did exist, and this should be a lesson for European man, suddenly crushed by the rise of the great powers, the emergence of capitalism and by the rapid spread of individualism – such is the message of More's *Utopia*.

All this was confirmed by the French pirates, Normans and Bretons, who began to appear in Guanabara in 1504, only two years after Vespucci, and who went back to tell the tale. They said that when they came near to Rio, as soon as their ships got into the bay, they were surrounded by the Tupinambá canoes and greeted with VIP treatment. The natives went on board, caressed them, offered fruits and presents, and even gave them their women. Could anyone ask for more? Imagine these ravenous creatures, after months condemned to each other's company on the high seas and sometimes having to eat even the ship's rats, reaching a place where all they had to do was stretch out their hand to eat the most exotic delicacies. In the case of the women, they didn't even have to put out their hand: extremely well-groomed, with long tresses, firm breasts, stout thighs, robust bottoms, shaven in their intimate parts, and already naked – they flung themselves at them. It's not surprising that several of these sailors never went back to France. They preferred to stay here, in the shade of the Sugar Loaf, with as many wives as they could satisfy, procreating children galore, and treated as wizards of the highest order. Some of the French even followed the savages' example and adopted the practice of having a daily bath.

It is true that they only got this treatment because they were French. The Tupinambás, who had just been introduced to the Portuguese too, soon discovered who they preferred to root for as invaders. The Portuguese enslaved and tortured them and had not the least respect for their customs – they could only think of using them to cut cane and chop down as many as possible of the trees that produced a red dye – the so-called *pau-brasil* from which Brazil got its name. The French, on the other hand, who also had their eye on the *pau-brasil*, soon saw that it was a good idea to treat the natives well and indulge them – even if it was only to have them on their side in case Portugal should get seriously interested in Rio (in those early times, the Portuguese were blind to Guanabara, and fixed their sights on Bahia and Pernambuco to the north, and São Vicente to the south). This strategy worked, and there began a Franco-Tupinambá entente which would last some seventy years. Escorted by the Indian warriors, the French climbed off their ships, explored the beaches, penetrated the jungle, and, communicating by gestures and words, got on famously with the locals. By 1510, there were already bilingual people on either side – French who said: '*Te mutimúti, aruá, kybáb*!' ('I've got hooks, mirrors, combs!') and Indians who exclaimed: '*Bien sûr*!' and: '*Ou-là-là*!' Before it became Portuguese by law, Rio was *de facto* French.

Surprisingly, another Tupinambá speciality observed by the visitors didn't succeed in lowering their social prestige: cannibalism. Perhaps this was because their habit of eating human flesh was only motivated by revenge (it had nothing to do with meat shortages) and obeyed rigid rules of etiquette. First, they only ate their prisoners of war, and even then, only the strong and courageous – preferably the Temiminós, a tribe that they'd carried on a war with for so long (500 years) that it had almost become a sport. Secondly, nothing was done in a hurry: the prisoner had a series of rights and duties to accomplish before he died.

To begin with, the condemned man became the personal guest of the chief, who installed him in his own hut, where he was fed on the fat of the land. He was also obliged to marry a charming Tupinambá girl, and allowed to enjoy a decent honeymoon. No 'civilised' country treated its defeated enemies in such a way. The prisoner couldn't even think of trying to escape – it would be the height of shame for his tribe. On the day set for the execution, the neighbouring villages were called together for the feast, and came in huge numbers. After a lot of singing and dancing, the guests sat on the ground in a great circle. The prisoner was called into the middle, his body was painted and he was given stones and bits of pottery to throw at his captors. It was also part of the ceremony for him to curse them as vehemently as possible and swear that his brothers would avenge him. Just as he reached the climax, he got a hefty blow on the skull with a club, which smashed his cranium, just to teach him a lesson, and he died with a flourish, to the sound of applause and: 'Encore!'

Then his body was lovingly taken apart. The tougher parts were hung in front of a fire to smoke, and later given to the warriors; the brains, entrails and other viscera were cooked into a stew, which was served to the women; the blood, still warm, went to the children. For my readers, who doubtless prefer *escargots*, a *cassoulet* or a *bouillabaisse*, food like this might seem revolting. But the Tupinambás ate, drank and smacked their lips, and at the end of the meal felt stronger for having absorbed a powerful enemy. The meal, in fact, was almost symbolic. Because of the number of people present, the most each guest got was a toe or half an ear. The lunch itself must have consisted of armadillos, capybaras and wild peccaries, followed by quantities of *cauim* (fermented manioc juice) and a week's partying.

The French, who invent culinary masterpieces out of the strangest of ingredients, were the last to be shocked by the feeding habits of Rio's natives. So much so that their ships went back to the Channel carrying not only our first list of exports (Brazil wood, manioc flour, pepper, tobacco, monkeys, parrots), but also some specimens of 'natural man' – Tupinambás who embarked willingly, certain they were going 'to heaven'. And, so long as they didn't die on the voyage, in a sense they really were. When they got to Europe, the natives were pampered and indulged, much more than the monkeys and parrots, and were paraded naked in sumptuous 'Brazilian festivals' for the kings of France. Two of these festivals occurred in Rouen, in Normandy: one, in 1550, for King Henri II and his mistress Diane de Poitiers; the second in 1562 for the young Charles IX and the queen mother, Catherine de' Medici. At this second festival, one of the guests, notebook in hand, was Michel de Montaigne.

The Tupinambás can't have misbehaved either because, following the example of the French who stayed in Rio, some of them stayed in France for the rest of their lives, surviving the cold, learning the language, and (some of them) learning to distinguish between the 200 kinds of cheese. The majority went to work for the nobility in Paris, in domestic roles which forced them to wear silk stockings and wigs. The well-endowed (in every sense) even married the more daring Parisian girls and had children by them, the first cariocas born away from home. So, there was one moment, in the middle of the sixteenth century, in which the vision of a Tupinambá promenading in his long coat along the Rive Gauche was no more absurd than that of a Frenchman, naked, painted red and with a headdress, fishing with a bow and arrow on Flamengo beach – that was the way many Frenchmen lived around here, and some of them even enriched their diet by converting to anthropophagy.

A few years later, Europe would devour the travel books of two French religious men, the Franciscan friar André Thévet and the Calvinist theologian Jean de Léry, relating their experiences in Brazil between 1555 and 1560. At different times, both of them had been in Rio with the Vice-Admiral Nicolas Durand de Villegagnon, when he tried to found the nucleus of a French colony in the tropics. For religious reasons, Thévet and Léry couldn't stand one another. But both were fascinated, favourably and unfavourably, by our Indians and described their daily life in minute detail, with abundant pictures to illustrate it. Many writers were influenced by these books, among them Montaigne, one of the first people to see, in Rouen, some of the real-life specimens they were talking about. Montaigne also had a manservant who had been with Villegagnon in Rio – while he was brushing down his frock coats, the retainer told him intimate details of the natives' existence that might have escaped the attention of the writer/travellers.

In his essay 'On the Cannibals', which would be read all over the world, Montaigne compared the natives' social organisation to that of European civilisation. Montaigne would much sooner trust a native. To begin with, they didn't wage wars of conquest – unlike the Europeans, who were tearing each other apart for a few pints of the Atlantic

Ocean. They fought for nobler aims: honour, justice and revenge. If they were defeated, these savages didn't run like rabbits, they were brave to the last – they might be killed, but not defeated. Agreed, they were polygamists, but so what? The Bible was full of examples of civilisations that practised polygamy. And they didn't fight over inheritances, because for them, everything was common property, the land as much as the sea and the stars. In fact, Montaigne said, this primitive 'communism' was a godsend, and it was astonishing that it was being practised by barbarians. What was more, he went on, it would be a good idea to reconsider the concepts of 'barbarian' and 'savage', adopted by Europeans to refer to peoples they didn't know, and merely because they had different customs. And, he added, cannibalism itself, as practised in Guanabara, was more humane than the executions carried out in European religious wars, in which wounded prisoners were thrown to the beasts or buried alive.

In essence, that was what Montaigne said, causing much ink to be spilled. Like everything that came out of his pen, it had a profound effect on the thought of his time. In later times, too – the seventeenth century would use our Tupinambás as a platform for the theory of the 'natural goodness' of man. Man was good, the theory went; it was civilisation that had corrupted him. So civilisation had to change, and so should notions of rights, justice and property.

As the decades went by, the image of the Indians

of Guanabara bay was perfected by other writers. Now it was somewhat embarrassing to reveal that, contrary to the story the writer/travellers had disseminated throughout Europe, the Tupinambás were not exactly angels. They were always at war with their neighbours (fighting, in fact, was their work); they enslaved members of enemy tribes (and sold them to the white men); they did have certain forms of government, they had a legal system and were fully acquainted with private property. Even the supposed innocence of their women couldn't hide their sensuousness and the variety of sexual techniques at their command, which competed with those of Parisian courtesans – practice makes perfect, as we know.

But already in those days, if a legend had turned into a reality, they went on printing the legend. And the legendary Indian was better than the real one. Towards the end of the eighteenth century, Jean-Jacques Rousseau transformed him once and for all into the 'noble savage'. Free, equal and fraternal, just like the motto adopted by the French Revolution.

Pity that, long before this – after centuries of war, slavery, smallpox, alcoholism, hunger and Christianity – there wasn't a single Tupinambá left in Rio to savour his own achievements.

Come to that, I don't know how we didn't have *sans-culotte* cariocas with Phrygian caps at the fall of the Bastille. Because, if it had depended on that

sensitive sea-wolf Villegagnon, Rio would have
been French, *de facto* and *de jure*, from the sixteenth century on. With all the foreseeable consequences: our kings would have been Louises instead
of Pedros, we would have taken up cycling instead
of football, and we'd be eating duck with *langouste*
instead of *bife a cavalo* [steak 'on horseback', with
fried eggs on top] – all of which wouldn't have
stopped De Gaulle one day saying that we are not a
serious country. These things nearly happened, and
French men and women who today land in Rio on
some internal flight, disembarking at Santos-Dumont airport, can hardly imagine that, in a way,
they are walking on ground that once belonged to
them – and where struggles took place which are an
important part of French history.

Old Santos-Dumont, with its modernist terminal,
is one of the smallest and most attractive urban
airports in the world. It's right in the centre of the
city, and its runway starts three yards away from
the sea – just before it lands, the aircraft skims
over the waters of Guanabara bay. To anyone
watching the landing, it's as if the wheels were
going to touch the water first. Just as in a cartoon,
the runway is bordered with dwarf palms, and just
over the bay stands the Sugar Loaf, so the visitor
should be in no doubt that he's arriving in Rio. In
the past, before this part of the bay was infilled, the
whole area where the airport now is was French
territorial waters, round an island the Indians called
Serigipe, which was half a mile from land. It was on

this island (now the Naval College, linked to the airport by a small bridge), that on 10 November 1555, Villegagnon disembarked to create the nucleus of a colony in Brazil: Antarctic France.

If anyone was equipped for this task, it was Villegagnon, a brilliant soldier and precursor of geopolitics. A short time before his Brazilian adventure, he had achieved things to make the French cheer and leave the English furious. One of them, in 1548, was the kidnapping of Mary Stuart. The Catholic heir to the Scottish throne was barely five years old and, as was usual in the best royal families, her hand was already disputed by neighbouring thrones. The English King Henry VIII wanted to marry her to his son Edward VI, make her Queen of England and turn Scotland Protestant. The French King Henri II wanted to marry her to his son Francis II, to keep France and Scotland united by Catholicism. When they found out about the base intentions of the French, the English thought she would only be safe in London and sent an admiral to fetch her. But Villegagnon got there first: he circumvented the English fleet at Leith, picked Mary Stuart up in Dumbarton and took her to France. The English already wanted his guts for garters after this, but that wasn't all. In 1552, after protecting Malta against the Turks, Villegagnon defended the port of Brest against the English, which obtained him the title of Vice-Admiral of Brittany. And at his suggestion, France crowned its dominion over the Mediterranean by occupying the island of Corsica – not realising that, 230 years later, Napoleon would be born there. With all this to his credit, Villegagnon wasn't just a military man. He was also a shrewd diplomat, adroit in his dealing with kings and queens, and a friend of writers like Rabelais and Ronsard. And as if this wasn't enough, he was a theologian, versed in canon law.

In 1554, as he was sailing along the south-west coast of Brazil, Villegagnon realised that Guanabara, still abandoned by the Portuguese, was ripe for conquest. He went back to France, sold the idea to Henri II and Admiral Coligny, and they authorised him to take the area under his wing. A year later, with three ships and 600 men (some of them a personal retinue from Scotland), Villegagnon, now Viceroy of Brazil, arrived in Rio to the screams of macaws and parakeets.

He occupied the island of Serigipe, renamed it Coligny to please his superior in the French navy, and built a fort there, equipped with cannons taken from the ships. The natives, as he had foreseen, unhesitatingly flocked to his colours and helped him to build on the beach opposite – the future Flamengo beach – the first houses of a city to be called Henriville. Careful of etiquette among chieftains, Villegagnon made friends with the influential Tupinambá chief Cunhambebe. The two got on so well that they began to write a French/Tupi dictionary together. In a short time, the number of French ships going to and from Guanabara was very satisfactory, and everything pointed to Henri II himself having a holiday in the colony. What Villegagnon did not foresee was that his men would also become fanatical followers of the native women, and launch into a sexual militancy to frighten even the local parrots.

Villegagnon was terribly disgusted by this orgy, not for racial so much as religious reasons. Devout from head to toe, he had made a vow of chastity and kept it more faithfully than the pope. For him, sex outside marriage was anathema – which makes it hard to understand why he brought so few women with him on the expedition, and all of those were married or engaged to his officers. This was his first mistake in Antarctic France – because the greater part of his troops were young bachelors full of life, let loose in an orchard of native women sent wild by their blue eyes. Villegagnon asked Cunhambebe to try to control the girls' urges. But for the chieftain (who was a man of the world) the idea was impractical – as well as, let's face it, a little naïve. Isolated, Villegagnon tried to oblige each of his men to limit themselves to one native and marry her, using the expedition's notary to officiate. The alternative was the gallows. The lads, once they knew that the marriage would still hold good in France, preferred to rebel, even if it cost them their lives – and it cost many of them just that. Others, more practical, merely fled to the back of the bay or secretly took ship back to Europe, as Montaigne's manservant must have done.

Two years later, in 1557, the number of defections by flight or hanging got so worrying that Villegagnon realised how precarious the situation was. To make Henriville a real city, he needed professional soldiers who could defend it and civilians, men and women, to populate it. For this reason, he wrote to Coligny asking for help. But Coligny, an ex-Catholic, had converted to Swiss Calvinism, the dissident form of Protestantism which was beginning to make inroads in France and which was being harshly repressed. Coligny saw the possibility of making Antarctic France into a Calvinist colony, and instead of the soldiers and ordinary citizens Villegagnon had asked him for, sent him a batch of preachers and about 300 adherents to the new sect, all of them fat, flushed, with thin lips and penetrating little eyes. Villegagnon had to swallow his reluctance – he had no option, and anyway, the Calvinists brought capital with them to invest in the new land.

So on a humble island in Rio, with no water and no home comforts, there began a religious quarrel whose perfect setting would have been the Renaissance salons of Europe, among freshly painted Tintorettos and Gutenberg first editions – but here, in the jungle, it did seem a trifle out of place. With the fort surrounded by cannibals (very well-behaved ones, but cannibals nevertheless), and under the permanent threat of attack from the Portuguese, the colonists of Antarctic France spent the day in heated discussions about the rites of the

Eucharist – the Catholics saying that the wine was literally Christ's blood transubstantiated, the Protestants saying it was just symbolic. In the middle, Villegagnon, trying to reconcile the two factions, only managed to alienate both: the Catholics accused him of having sold out to the Calvinists, and they in their turn accused him of playing a double game. There was an outbreak of disorder, an attempt to assassinate Villegagnon, and the once shrewd Viceroy ordered more people on either side to be hanged. This soured things in Antarctic France; you could have cut the atmosphere with a knife. In 1560, Villegagnon decided to go to Paris to explain the situation to Henri II.

As if they'd been waiting for him to go, the Portuguese, led by Governor-General Mem de Sá, came from Bahia and attacked and destroyed Fort Coligny. But, unable to defend the island, they left, and the French and the Tupinambás retook their positions on the beaches and islands. Villegagnon, following everything from a distance and with a time-lag, could have come back. But, depressed and disappointed, he decided to stay in Europe while his nephew, Captain Bois le Comte, took charge of the colony. Four years later the Portuguese, now commanded by the nobleman Estácio de Sá, and reinforced by the Temiminós (enemies of the Tupinambás), returned to the attack. The Tupinambás came out to sea in 180 canoes to defend the settlement, but in vain. The Portuguese razed Henriville to the ground, and occupied the strategic *morro* Cara de Cão [Dog's Face], next to the Sugar Loaf. And, in case there should be any doubt, they did what their predecessors should have done from the start: on 1 March 1565, they founded a city there. It was a village to which Estácio gave the name of the City of St Sebastian of Rio de Janeiro, in homage to the King of Portugal and the saint riddled with arrows – it's said that St Sebastian himself was seen in the battle, jumping from boat to boat on the high seas and terrorising the Tupinambás. It was only then that Rio became truly Portuguese and colonisation began.

But don't imagine things quietened down at this point. The French survivors and the Tupinambás kept up resistance on the *morros* and, for the next five years, any Portuguese who dared to go up to the Glória or Santa Teresa *morros* risked getting filled with lead from an arquebus or shot through by a stray arrow. The story of Estácio de Sá was the best. In the final battle on Glória, on 20 January 1567 – ironically, St Sebastian's Day – his cheek was scratched by a poisoned arrow. But unlike the saint, whose supernatural powers allowed him to survive arrow wounds, Estácio, with something of the tragic Siegfried about him, died a month later, and so became Guanabara's first martyr.

Rio gave his name to a neighbourhood – Estácio – where, 360 years after his death, the city's most typical product took on its definitive shape: the samba. Which just about sums the matter up. With all this chaos right at its beginning, Rio has a strong penchant for the epic – and an even stronger penchant, thank God, for the epic to end in samba.

For 500 years Europe has been trying to civilise us, without much success. In the seventeenth century, the Rio coastline had daily visits from French, English, Dutch and Spanish pirates – though education was hardly uppermost in their minds. At Cabo Frio, Paraty or Angra dos Reis, wherever there was a quiet little cove and an Indian or a white man disposed to trade, they appeared, and the process of exchanging raw materials for coloured trinkets began, until the Portuguese came and put a stop to it. But there were always some buccaneers left behind, their doublets filthy with the droppings of the parrot on their shoulder, prime candidates, who knows, for stories like *Treasure Island* and *Moonfleet*. A pity we had no Robert Louis Stevenson or J. Meade Falkner to write them. It's not for lack of a backdrop in the Rio landscape.

Almost the whole city lay next to sordid warehouses. Where Gamboa now is, there were taverns frequented by footloose Europeans, including suspicious-looking gypsies, where *cachaça* was served and smuggling was the rule. Because it was riddled with quiet little inlets, Guanabara bay was infested with whales who used it for mating. When they saw a lot of water spurting up behind a stone, the locals knew it was whales making love. Unconcerned about interrupting their pleasure, and with no notion of a close season, they stuck them full of harpoons. The ships left Rio loaded with the meat, whalebone and blubber for oil; what was left over was used for food and lighting some of the houses. There were so many whales that a government edict of 1619 obliged the suppliers to get rid of the innards out at sea, to prevent the stink in the city. The whales took a while to realise that these were dangerous waters and only much later, perhaps just for lack of quorum, they stopped coming here. Nowadays, only the odd stray finds its way onto the beach at Ipanema or Barra da Tijuca. It's received, not by harpooners, but by television crews.

Just like today, cariocas might die of all kinds of things in those times, but not of boredom. In 1663, the Portuguese built in Rio the largest ship of the century: the *Padre Eterno* [Eternal Father], a galleon 180 feet long, with six bridges and 180 cannons, which could hold 4,000 men. It was so huge that the point on the Ilha do Governador where it was launched became known as the Ponta do Galeão (it's where the international airport now is). They must have needed ships as big as this for all the variety and quantity of merchandise being exported from Rio: sugar, rum, wood, tobacco, whale oil, animals, and then, suddenly, gold – which was discovered inland in Minas Gerais just before 1700, and which began to flow to Europe through Guanabara. Because of it the French turned their eyes to Brazil again, and King Louis XIV, worried about the friendship between Portugal and England, decided to attack Rio. This time, it wasn't just piracy, it was an act of war.

On the first onslaught, in August 1710, the commander Jean-François Duclerc, knowing he couldn't get past the forts at the bay's entrance, disembarked some distance away, at Guaratiba, and decided to invade on foot, from the interior. For a week, guided by an ex-slave with a grudge against the Portuguese, about 1,000 Frenchmen marched through the jungles of Jacarepaguá and Tijuca towards the city, unmolested. There was something absurd about pirates invading the city on foot, but even so, the Portuguese Governor Castro Morais, scared out of his wits, shut himself in his palace and left the post of Commander of the Troops to St Anthony – yes, the saint, famous for his achievements as a marriage-broker, and dead since 1231. Appointed defender of the city, even though it was a bit out of his normal line of business, St Anthony came up trumps: when he saw that the troops were immobilised, he inspired the carioca people to resist, and they were brilliant.

As soon as they got to Lapa near the centre of the city, the French – more dead than alive, after a forty-mile hike – found themselves in a trap. The population attacked them from above, out of windows, with firearms, boiling oil, metal pans, stones and any objects that came to hand. There were armed conflicts in the Ruas do Riachuelo, Ajuda and São José. When the French entered the present-day Rua Primeiro de Março to take the Governor's palace (on the spot where the Banco do Brasil Cultural Centre now stands), the invaders were greeted with shots from the students of the Jesuit College. Only then did the Governor get his courage back and dispatched the cavalry and the rest of the forces to capture the survivors. When the smoke cleared, 400 French had died, 200 were wounded and another 400 were prisoners. For seven days, the city danced and sang.

Among the prisoners was Commander Duclerc. He was a respectable officer, with a plume in his hat, not a fifth-rate pirate. As a prisoner of war, he didn't like the lodgings reserved for him in the Jesuit monastery and demanded to be treated as a nobleman. The Governor agreed and put him up in a Brazilian lieutenant's house, on the corner of the Rua da Quitanda and the Rua do Sabão, under heavy guard. In March 1711, Duclerc was killed in this house by three men in cloaks, who, so it seems, had got past the guard with no difficulty. The business was never cleared up, but rumour had it that there had been an affair between the lieutenant's wife and the French gallant. Back in Paris, Duclerc's widow was furious, and blamed Rio's Governor for the crime. Louis XIV was even less pleased, and vowed revenge. He kept his vow: seven months later, the fleet of Admiral René Duguay-Trouin entered Guanabara bay – to burn the place down, literally.

This was the greatest, and perhaps the only, defeat in Rio's history – not counting, of course,

Uruguay's victory over Brazil, 2–1, right here in the Maracanã stadium, in the World Cup final in 1950. On 20 September of that same year, 1711, Duguay-Trouin arrived in the city with seventeen ships, 285 officers, 5,551 men and 600 cannon. The carioca fortresses opened fire against the invaders, but in a few hours Duguay-Trouin managed to get all his ships into the bay. Undefended, the Brazilian ships of war anchored by the docks were burnt, gunpowder deposits were blown up, and the convents neutralised. When the shooting was over, Duguay-Trouin sent a message full of demands to the Portuguese Governor: he wanted satisfaction for the death of Duclerc, the freeing of the prisoners from the previous invasion, the surrender of the city and reimbursement of his expedition's expenses – in other words, Rio would have to pay for being invaded. The Governor sent a lukewarm, temporising reply. The Admiral was not satisfied, and *malgré lui* ordered the bombardment.

On the night of 20 September, during one of the most violent storms Rio has ever seen, the batteries armed by the French in the fortresses they had captured opened fire. Terror was let loose. The cannon shots mixed with the rain, thunder and lightning sounded like a rehearsal for the Last Judgement. The Governor and the militia bolted. With no one to defend it, the population abandoned the city too, taking whatever they could along the abandoned roads. Next morning, with no resistance, hundreds of French soldiers appeared in the mud-ridden streets and sacked houses and stores – against the orders of Duguay-Trouin, who had forbidden looting, and had made examples of some of the perpetrators by executing them. When they thought the danger was over, the people came back, and, sharing their contempt for the inept Governor, got on well with the French, even negotiating with them. Almost two months later, the Governor liquidated the Treasury and paid a heavy ransom in gold, silver, sugar and oxen. Also, to the joy of the cariocas, the Portuguese traders had to buy back, with ninety-seven per cent interest, the sixty merchant ships Duguay-Trouin had captured. Only then did the corsair give the city back and leave. The next day, as always, Rio awoke to the sound of singing.

Beyond the somewhat unsubtle means sometimes used by Europeans to civilise us during these five centuries, another factor has always got in the way of these attempts: the cariocas themselves.

The word itself is Indian and there are various versions of its origins. The most commonly accepted refers to a stone house (*cari-oca*, the white man's house), built in 1503 where the present-day Ruas Barão do Flamengo and Paissandu meet (next to Flamengo beach) by a Portuguese left behind by Gonçalo Coelho's expedition. The stream that rises on the Corcovado, runs through Laranjeiras and enters the bay there also took this name. According to the natives, its waters were responsible for the beauty of their songs and chants. In later centuries, the governors of the city channelled it, so that streets passed over ninety-nine per cent of its course and it became almost invisible. I myself spent a good part of my childhood, in the fifties, where those two streets meet, and I've never seen a drop of it.

By carioca, we mean those born in the city, who are *cariocas da gema* [from the yolk of the egg], as well as those born anywhere else, but who live here and identify with Rio's *jeito* [its indefinable spirit], and become part of the city and make it even more characteristic. A cat born in an oven isn't a biscuit, as our proverb says, and so there are real cariocas born in Bahia, Amazonia, Berlin, Copenhagen, Tunis. By *jeito* we mean, among other things, an almost masochistic refusal to take oneself very seriously, a combination of boredom and mockery in the face of any kind of power, and, not least, a *joie de vivre* which defies any kind of rational argument. A carioca could never be Swiss, but a Swiss might be able to become carioca, if Rio is given time to seduce him and, in the good sense of the word, corrupt him.

Rio is a great corrupter of adults. French, Portuguese, English, Italians, Spaniards, Germans, even Scandinavians, as well as Arabs and Jews of various nationalities, have all come over here in waves and laid down roots – for foreign surnames that have been here for centuries, the Rio and Manhattan phone books are in competition. In a short time, these immigrants have lost their European starch and acquired the cool, the typically carioca ease, and so are blessed with something that, here, is considered an achievement: loss of nationality.

The Rio French stopped being French and became cariocas (Duguay-Trouin would have become a carioca and a half, if he'd not come on business). Rio's Italians never were Italians – they felt carioca as soon as they got off the boat: it's hardly worth saying that the same goes for the Portuguese, once the natural resentments between coloniser and colonised had been surmounted (the mulatto women made their contribution, softening an enormous number of them). Even Ronald Biggs, the infamous English gangster, was 'corrupted': in the twenty-eight years he lived here, he became a popular, well-loved figure in the neighbourhood of Santa Teresa. He married a mulatta, became a Flamengo fan and not only learnt to speak perfect Portuguese, he became an expert in carioca slang – his television interviews were priceless.

Rio is a synthesis, not an agglomeration. That's how it was in the nineteenth and twentieth centuries, and that's how it still is. Any immigrant's children are born as carioca as can be, instilled with know-how for the beach, for chatting on street corners, and for having a draught beer with a bite to eat in the local bar. As the generations succeed one another, the memory of their foreign ancestors becomes more ectoplasmic, and is replaced by that of their carioca parents or grandparents. This is even the case with the Jews; among them are, still today, some of the best scholars to have investigated Rio's history.

In the old Centre of the city, there's an area called Saara [Sahara]. It has nothing to do with camels, oases with palm-trees or scimitars – it's the acronym of a commercial organisation, SAARA, meaning the Society of Friends [Amigos] of the Area of the Rua da Alfândega. This comprises a labyrinth of eleven streets, with about 1,500 little businesses, restaurants, textile shops, jewellers, spice emporia, and bazaars full of knick-knacks. It's one of the few places in Rio where you can say that certain ethnic groups predominate: in this case, Arab and Jewish shopkeepers. Things have been that way for a long time, but the institution was only founded in 1962, fourteen years after the creation of the state of Israel. That's to say, while in the Middle East the traumatic division of Palestine, with the consequences we all know about, was coming into being, their carioca cousins declared themselves to be friends and joined together to buy and sell. Decades have gone by and, out there, not very far from the real Sahara, they're still throwing missiles and car-bombs at one another. In Rio's Saara, Arabs and Jews tell jokes at the shop door, share *kibbes* and samosas at lunchtime, and, at Carnival or World Cup time, get together even more avidly to sell feathers or sequins for costumes, or Brazilian team shirts. In fact, it's not right to call them Arabs and Jews. They're just cariocas, just as the Koreans who have recently begun to compete with them for the area's commerce will soon be.

This is a Rio phenomenon – I'm less sure about the rest of Brazil. In the south of the country, many people of German, Polish or Italian extraction live in well-defined colonies, snubbing one another, even if they've been there for three or four generations. But Rio, historically, has got used to welcoming people from everywhere, and encouraging a wonderful mixture. If Shakespeare had been carioca, he would never have written *Romeo and Juliet*, even if the story had been about the daughter of a Flamengo fan and the son a Vasco fan.

Many cariocas whose names are well known outside Brazil have at least one European grandfather. But who could care less about the grandfather? Not even the grandmother. The ancestors of the composer and conductor Heitor Villa-Lobos were Spanish. Bossa nova composer and songwriter Tom Jobim's were French and Dutch, and modernist architect Oscar Niemeyer's, German. The father of the big shot João Havelange, who dominated FIFA for twenty-four years, was Belgian (and avoided dying in the *Titanic* by missing the boat in Southampton). But no one can beat the ultra-carioca Carmen Miranda, whose name became a synonym for Brazil in American films of the time of the Second World War and who, as everyone knows, was Portuguese by birth. And there are plenty more examples. Their talent might have been in their genes, but their lifestyle – which, in the end, is what influenced their creativity – was typical of Rio.

Being descended from Europeans, you'd have expected them to keep a minimum of the composure inherited from their grandparents, right? Wrong. Villa-Lobos's grandfather would have been proud of his grandson's fame, thought of, as he is, as the greatest composer of the Americas. But perhaps he would be shocked to find out that what Villa-Lobos really enjoyed was playing the piano in the brothels in the Lapa, playing snooker with the local spivs, dressing like them and hanging around with the musicians of *choro* bands. What would Niemeyer's Prussian ancestors think if they saw him in his underpants, in his office in Copacabana, greeting the representatives of important international organisations who had come to ask him for designs for their headquarters? What are we to say of Jobim, who played hard to get with American producers who besieged him, but could be found by any passer-by in the bars in Leblon? A foreigner would never believe that these renowned – and thus 'inaccessible' – men walked around the streets of Rio like ordinary citizens. For them, however, it was the most natural thing in the world, and when they did it, they were merely practising one of the best of carioca attributes: simplicity. Rio reduces everyone, whatever their origin, their fame or social class, to a shirt worn outside the trousers, a battered pair of bermudas and a pair of flip-flops.

The carioca writer Paulo Coelho has already

sold, at the last count, fifty million copies of his books in fifty-five languages. Between one book and another, he spends his time being paid homage to by crowned heads and getting telephone calls from cardinals, grand viziers, ayatollahs, *candomblé* priests and other religious leaders, who all read him. Well, until a short time ago, even though he was a best-seller on a planetary scale, Paulo lived in a ground-floor flat in the Rua Raimundo Correa, a busy pedestrian thoroughfare in Copacabana. When he needed to, he went out to buy matches or biros in the bar opposite his building, mixing with winos, comb-sellers and general passers-by. Everyone knew who he was and no one bothered him. Three or four years ago, Paulo moved to a building on the Avenida Atlântica, still in Copacabana, but hasn't given up his habit of strolling along the wide pavement parallel to the sea, where no one except friends approaches him. Many know him from the time when he was a tireless record-producer, and know that, in essence, the only visible change in his life is that, because of his books, he's become famous from Patagonia to Cochinchina.

Someone else who can often be seen, only this time along by the beach in Leblon, is the composer Chico Buarque. Women from all over Brazil say publicly they would faint just from being in his presence. In Rio, no one seems to be much affected when they see Chico in the street with his grandson in a pushchair – at most, they give him a surreptitious look of burning desire. Another national institution, the singer-composer Caetano Veloso, goes to the beach opposite his apartment on Avenida Vieira Souto, in Ipanema – the same place he's frequented since the beginning of his career, when he didn't even dream of living at that address. No crowds gather round him on the beach. Romário, the star footballer, at the peak of his career as centre-forward for the Brazilian team, who were world champions in 1994, when Romário was voted their best player that year, could be watched playing foot-volleyball daily with his teammates, with a net set up on the beach at Barra da Tijuca, without interrupting the enjoyment of the nearby bathers. And Ronaldo, his successor, plays for Real Madrid but spends his free time in Rio, without causing any fuss. Rio includes everyone in its way of life, and nobody pays much attention to celebrities.

Not that cariocas are snobs. They're just not easily bedazzled. Long familiarity with power has bred a natural indifference to the powerful, whether they're politicians, millionaires, or media icons. One of the rare exceptions was the then sex symbol of the universe, Brigitte Bardot, when she was here in 1964. At first, Bardot's presence nearly caused a riot in Copacabana, and she didn't even dare to appear at her hotel window. But the city got used to her, and a few days later, when she came into a nightclub, you could already hear the comments: 'Oh God, here's Brigitte *again*!' Orson Welles spent six months in Rio in 1942, shooting a film, *It's All True*. The revolutionary *Citizen Kane*, released a year before, had made him the greatest name in cinema, but Orson walked round the city indistinguishable from the landscape, except when he sometimes threw his money around – and the furniture out of his hotel bedroom. *It's All True* was never finished, but Orson left behind some marks of his time in Rio: he invented a drink, 'Samba in Berlin' – *cachaça* with Coke – which was in fashion for a while. In 1970, Janis Joplin, who'd just become a legend at Woodstock, also came here and forgot to leave. One day, she had a skinful with a gang of young people in a square in Ipanema and keeled over. The lads borrowed a shaving brush, soap and a razor from a local barber and, taking advantage of her unconsciousness, shaved off the famous balls of hair in her armpits. There have been no cases of foreign celebrities who've been followed round the city by paparazzi and had their clothes torn. OK, so there was one Carnival when Jayne Mansfield's breasts popped out of her décolletage at a ball at the Copacabana Palace, and, by chance, there was a photographer on the lookout. But maybe Jayne's breasts wanted to take a look at the dancers.

Rio always treats visitors with affection, but, during its long career as the nation's capital, it soon learned not to trust its rulers. Between 1565 and 1960, there lived and worked here fifty-three Captain-Governors, seven Viceroys, a mad Queen, a Prince Regent (who later became king), two Emperors and eighteen Presidents of the Republic –

sufficient evidence for cariocas to be persuaded that, with a few exceptions, everyone in power deserves to have a donkey's tail appended to his frock coat. Many of them, born in the provinces, profited from the veneer of civilisation the city gave them – along with other benefits – after removing the grime. In exchange, they've not helped Rio so much as helped themselves to it. But the city always got its own back: making fun of them in jokes that made their way round the whole country, and always defeating them in the next elections. There's only one thing more difficult than getting elected to any post in Rio, from President of the Republic to caretaker of an apartment-block: getting re-elected.

Cariocas' impatience with their rulers isn't limited to human beings. For some reason, a mayor of Rio in the early nineties had to make a series of visits to the city's zoo. Every time, he was a target for the droppings of the well-loved ape Tião, one of the zoo's major attractions. These animals usually do this to the public, but Tião was selective. When he saw a group of VIPs and reporters by his cage, the chimp armed himself with his home-made balls and concentrated his efforts on the mayor. Next morning, the papers had a field day – because Tião was doing what many ordinary people would have liked to have done. As a reward, he got a vote in the next elections larger than that of several veteran politicians.

A collection of clichés besmirches the image of the carioca. For example, they say that cariocas don't work, spend their days on the beach, and can't go past a street corner or a bar without stopping to chat to someone they've just met for the first time, and who's already their firm friend. Other clichés are that cariocas are incapable of arriving on time for an appointment, they leave everything till the last minute, and their idea of making a date is to say: 'See you sometime.' Well, it's all true. But these features of our character, always thrust in our faces by non-cariocas, have an explanation – and, what's more, they often have their justifications.

First off, it's not true that cariocas don't work much. On the contrary, Rio is one of the Brazilian cities where people work most. Maybe it's the one where most is achieved. According to Brazil's main institute for national statistics, cariocas work forty hours and forty-seven minutes per week, an enviable average for any great world city – compare it with your own city. But they're not to blame if there are 127 hours and thirteen minutes left not to work. And this time, which in other cities is given over to sleeping or watching TV, cariocas use for doing much better things, like going to the beach, popping over to the local bar, having a good long natter, playing some form of sport – as practically every carioca does – or wandering round the streets. Rio is so full of choices that every hour of work ought to be counted twice – because, while he's working, the carioca has denied him or herself all these other things.

Then there's the backdrop. In other cities, it

might be a relief to spend the day between four walls, so as not to see one's surroundings. But in Rio, it's torture to be imprisoned in an office with a view over Guanabara bay or the Atlantic Ocean – you have the feeling that life is going on outside, and the duty to be done in exchange for one's salary is sheer agony. I can say this because I spent years working as an editor for the now defunct magazine *Manchete*, right opposite Burle Marx's sunlit gardens in Flamengo park, watching in the distance the boats sailing out of the Glória marina with young men in yachting-caps and girls in short shorts, off for adventures that made me dream of salt, sex and champagne – with the extra torture that sometimes I had to write the captions for reports on these same adventures.

So we can see that the ratio between forty hours and forty-seven minutes of work and 127 hours, thirteen minutes of leisure is, in Rio, profoundly wise. But, for someone looking at it objectively, the relationship is a deceptive one – because at the same time as cariocas can't be seen working (shut up as they are in offices, government institutions and commercial establishments), everyone can see cariocas *not* working. There's no way they can't be seen – because all leisure in Rio happens in the open air, in the public gaze, on beaches and the pavements alongside them, in squares, in the hundreds of street-side bars or hang-outs to be found on any corner. It's the kind of fun that happens in the street, and, as such, it's cheap or free, within everyone's reach.

The key word is 'street'. Cariocas have had a long love affair with it. They feel at home in the street. This is even reflected in the literature produced here in the last 150 years. Rio's main writers of fiction – Manuel Antônio de Almeida, Machado de Assis, Lima Barreto, Marques Rebelo, Nelson Rodrigues, Carlos Heitor Cony – were always attentive observers of the city's action. Rio might even have been the inventor of a literary genre: the *crônica*, a short and only apparently trivial narrative, written for newspapers and magazines, mixing up reality, fiction and comment, and whose setting is almost always the street (or at the very least, a window). The greatest of *cronistas*, Rubem Braga, fathered a number of excellent followers – Paulo Mendes Campos, Fernando Sabino, Elsie Lessa, José Carlos Oliveira – and the tradition is still kept going by writers like Aldir Blanc, Heloisa Seixas, and Joaquim Ferreira dos Santos. The *cronistas* are the city's antennae, the first to feel a change in the wind. They are also the ones who immortalise ordinary citizens, with more substance and surprises to them than many big names. And these people can only be found in the street.

Except for certain places and times to be avoided out of simple common sense, Rio is an invitation to a pedestrian. There's always something to see – maybe it's the fascinating variety of architecture, the mischievous charm of its human fauna, or the endless procession of female bodies. It's a city so receptive to being walked around that, when you think about it, there's no sense in fixing formal appointments in claustrophobic hideaways, no need for that First World obsession for the day and the time set in stone in one's diary. That's the reason for: 'See you sometime' – and they really do see each other. In the street, meetings last for as long as they have to; hour on hour or just a few minutes, and no one takes the huff when someone says he's got to get going. As for the fact that cariocas feel they're the firm friend of someone they've just met, it's because they are, by their very nature, open and confiding, and who's to criticise them? The opposite would be not liking someone a priori, turning away from them or mistrusting them at first sight, and becoming permanently embittered.

Ah, the beaches. Outsiders think that cariocas are never off them. It is true that, whatever time you go through Copacabana or Ipanema, even on a Tuesday at three in the afternoon, the sands are full of people. But who can be so sure they're cariocas? Some might be – students on holiday, OAPs, unemployed adults and chronic layabouts. Most probably, however, they are mostly tourists, international or Brazilian, who have the legal right to stretch out in the sun whenever they like. If you want to catch a real carioca on the beach during the week, you'd better try less orthodox times of the day. Lunchtime, for instance: for anyone who works a few blocks away from the sea, it's the ideal time for a dip (the lifeguard posts have showers to get rid of the salt). Or in the late afternoon, after office hours – especially between November and March when, with the clocks put forward, night only begins to fall at about eight o'clock. The most common thing, however, is for cariocas to get up early, whatever time they went to bed, and run or walk on the beach before going to work.

An advertisement about Rio published some time ago said: 'Come and live in the city where you'd like to spend your holidays.' In the photo, spread across a double page of the papers and magazines: a heart-stopping vision of the beaches at sunrise. But try to explain a carioca's relationship with the beach. It's not like the Americans on the California coast, or the French in the Côte d'Azur – places which, to be enjoyed, demand long-range planning, six months saving up and the car with wife, children, dog and a huge amount of luggage, all for two weeks' holiday. In places like that, people take a trip to the beach, as if they were going to a hotel in the mountains, or another country. In Rio, people just go to the beach, like going to the cinema, the shops or the bank – because it's there, twenty-four hours a day, all year round, and with an entire city round it, all its services fully available.

Here, the beach isn't just a towel for spreading out in the sun. It's a whole culture. You go to the beach to read the paper, meet friends, play foot-volleyball, get to know people, get the latest gossip and even, sometimes, to talk business. It's a space as natural as a town square, a restaurant or an office. It's part of daily existence, and nobody is the object of moral judgements because they are always tanned. Cariocas' bronze colour might mean a future skin cancer – but not, necessarily, laziness or unemployment.

Apart from that, it's unfair to accuse the beach of interfering with the terrific capacity for work the inhabitants of Rio display. At any hour of any day, trained observers can detect real cariocas running in Copacabana, walking in Ipanema, playing football in the little pitches on Flamengo park, rowing in Rodrigo de Freitas lagoon, fishing off the sea wall at Urca, surfing on Macumba beach, trekking in Tijuca forest, diving off the Cagarra islands, walking at Paineiras, hang-gliding off Pedra Bonita, practising *capoeira* in the Rocinha favela, pedalling along the cycle route that goes from Leblon to Santos-Dumont airport, and even scaling the Corcovado.

Whatever they might be doing, cariocas are only exercising what they think is their right. It's a right that should be the sacred duty of any great city: to let itself be owned and used by its citizens, and when it comes down to it, to let them feel themselves to be alive.

More or less as the Tupinambás of Rio felt in 1502.

CHAPTER TWO

In May 1992, a month away from the biggest meeting of ruling heads of state of all time, there were some who were wondering if it had been a good idea on the UN's part to choose Rio to host it. It was the United Nations Conference on the Environment and Human Development – the name was far too long to fit into headlines, and the media soon cut it down to Rio-92. It was an Earth Summit, a global ecological forum, a proposal for cleaning up the planet. For eleven days, the city would welcome the representatives of 190 nations, including 117 heads of state and Prime Ministers, with their huge numbers of staff and their perks, as well as 22,000 people linked to 9,000 non-governmental organisations (NGOs) and 4,000 foreign journalists. All the plans had been laid for it to run smoothly – but who could swear nothing would go wrong? And if something did, who would mop up afterwards?

Knowing of Rio's reputation for informality, they were frightened that the American President, George Bush (senior), would have his jacket-sleeve pulled by some barefoot urchin trying to sell fruit-drops. Or the British Prime Minister John Major, invited to a *macumba* ceremony and being possessed by the spirits. Or the French President François Mitterand, brought face-to-face with a *caracu com ovo* – an awful concoction of cheap black beer with a raw egg – in a corner bar. Or the Cuban dictator Fidel Castro having a bit of his beard cut off as a practical joke. Anything like that could happen.

But what really worried the director of the UN's office in Rio, the Argentine Aurelio Ruiz, were the installations of the Riocentro, the vast convention centre in Jacarepaguá chosen for the conference. A few days before the opening, which was to take place on 3 June, nothing was ready: the auditorium, meeting rooms, press office, communications centre, restaurants, bars. The jumble of wood, glass, wires, telephones, computers and furniture in boxes was terrifying. The companies with the job of putting up the set wouldn't get the work done if they were given six months, thought Ruiz. The blame would surely fall on the Rio office, for which he was responsible – but he didn't realise how the city worked.

'Don't worry, Sr. Ruiz,' said one of his assistants. 'It'll be like the samba schools at Carnival. Half an hour before each school comes in, nobody thinks they'll get their act together for the procession. There's chaos everywhere. Thousands of people in a state of disorder, each wing out of touch with the next one, folks wandering round in a complete daze, everyone knocking back the booze in the middle of the street, with every costume on you can imagine. Suddenly, someone blows a whistle. The people get in groups by costume, each wing fits into its allotted place, the drums begin to beat and the school emerges onto the avenue, wonderful as always. That's the way it is, every year. You'll see.'

Ruiz went pale. How could a UN employee dare to compare a conference that size with a samba procession?

But that was exactly what happened. Days later, someone blew a whistle, the teams got moving, the rooms and auditoriums were set up, and, on the eve of the opening, the Riocentro was just as it ought to be. Ruiz breathed again. For the eleven days of the congress, everything went according to plan. No carioca let the side down in front of the gringos. Neither did Bush, Major, Mitterand, Fidel and the others, in front of the cariocas. And while the great powers were swapping recipes for saving the world, Rio put on its own late-autumn show, giving suggestions for what an ideal world would be like: beautiful days, luminous nights, gently flowing traffic, complete peace in the streets (guaranteed by the army), not a gangster to be seen (where had they all gone?), not even a dog peeing on a lamppost.

The only dirt was the vast amount of rubbish left behind daily in the Riocentro by the delegates, whose aim it was to clean up the whole world.

But the carioca bin-men worked tirelessly and one of them, Ivanilson dos Santos, found a wallet with 3,000 dollars in it, mislaid by a Japanese ecologist. The wallet was returned to its owner. On the same day another bin-man, Jailson Fernandes, beat him: he found a bag belonging to a Frenchman containing 30,000 dollars – the equivalent of thirteen years of work for Jailson. The bag was handed back too. The bin-men got medals. Months later, in an official report, the UN would classify Rio-92 as 'the best-organised conference in its history'.

It must have been. But Rio wasn't particularly proud of the fact. If you wanted something really difficult, how about the samba-school procession that same year, a few months before, when the floats belonging to the Viradouro school, a reproduction of Red Square in Moscow, had literally burst into flames in the middle of the avenue?

Nobody can understand Rio without understanding Carnival. But which one? For the travel agencies, it's the samba-school procession – almost 60,000 people, black and white, in costume – which takes nineteen hours, divided between two nights, to cover the 700 yards of the Sambodrome. Cariocas know that the best Carnival in Rio takes place outside the Sambodrome, but the tourists who do come for the spectacle have nothing to complain about. They watch a show on a Godzilla scale, an opera in the open air in which, merely in terms of its creativity, sumptuousness and opulence, one of the main schools easily outdoes any of three or four Broadway musicals combined. Just the percussion sections (a minimum of twenty-nine bass-drums, thirty side-drums, forty-three kettle-drums, ten *cuícas*, seventy-seven tambourines, four *agogôs*, four washboards and ninety-two maracas – per school) are capable of producing somersaults and revolutions in the internal organs of the people in the stands.

But any particularly enthusiastic tourist can do even better: they can be one of the 60,000 heroes of the Sambodrome. In the package deal, which includes a flight, hotel and tickets for the stands, many tourist agencies abroad also sell the right to 'parade' with a school, costume provided. The tourists don't even have to know how to dance the samba because, as in old Busby Berkeley films, even the clumsiest of *gringas* isn't noticed. The norm, however, as in any spectacle, is that the parade is something you pay to sit down and watch.

Two hundred, a hundred, or even fifty years ago, the Rio Carnival was different. Nobody had to pay, nobody sat down and, instead of watching, every participant got their own fancy dress and celebrated his or her own Carnival. The spectacle was the city – all of it. It spread through every neighbourhood for days and nights, and its protagonists were the whole population. It was freedom, madness, endless larking about. As long as the party went on, moral standards valid for the rest of the year were suspended – solidly respectable breadwinners and civil servants went out on the Saturday night and only reappeared on Ash Wednesday; tired, happy, their necks imprinted with lipstick. Distinctions between rich and poor, saints and sinners, even between men and women, no longer existed. Nobody belonged to anyone: an expression, 'a Carnival love', summed up the fleeting passions that flared up in these few days; another, 'Carnival children', designated the consequences of these passions. The proof that, during Carnival, real life was put on hold is that, in a country as politically turbulent as Brazil in the nineteenth and twentieth centuries, no one *ever* dared to carry out a *coup d'état* in February – there wouldn't have been a quorum.

Year by year, Carnival evolved; its development accompanies the history of the city itself. Each influenced the other and helped to form the character of the carioca population. Or, to put it another way, to deform it. But the process took time. In the seventeenth and eighteenth centuries, when Brazil was still Portuguese and Rio was governed by viceroys, Carnival was the *entrudo*, as it was celebrated in Lisbon. This was a violent game, which spared neither old people, women, children, or the infirm. It consisted in one half of the population covering the other half in filth – throwing water, vinegar, eggs, flour, glue, lime, urine and other refuse over them – and vice versa, so both sides made a rubbish dump out of the whole city and thought that was just fine. It was dangerous to walk beneath a window: priests, policemen, official personages, whatever their uniform – if they didn't look out, they caught a pailful or a squirt of dirty water. They almost always returned the favour. At the end of Carnival, pneumonia abounded.

In the nineteenth century, when the Portuguese court was transferred to Rio in 1808 and independence came in 1822, the new Brazilian élite began to take their inspiration from more cultivated carnivals, like those of Nice and Venice. In 1840, there were already masked balls in Rio's hotels and theatres, enlivened by orchestras playing the latest rhythms from Europe: waltzes, polkas and quadrilles (these passing fashions lasted for decades in Brazil). Pierrots, Harlequins and Columbines filled the streets, along with the *zé-pereiras* – groups of people banging on drums, pans, cans or anything else that would make a noise. The Carnival clubs, called 'great societies', arose, which paraded sumptuous allegorical floats pulled along by pairs of horses, imitating the coaches that took the royal family to gala ceremonies – with the difference that, among the costumed merrymakers blowing kisses from the floats, there were near-naked women (prostitutes, naturally). Battles with flowers were staged, there was sea-bathing in Carnival costume and firework displays at the seaside. This was already Carnival as we know it, though it was still only for the whites, in harmony with a city that wanted to be European – which, in many senses, it really was.

But, in the middle of the nineteenth century, Rio

was also obviously African, with half its population consisting of blacks, both slave and free. And they had their own Carnival, much more creative and lively, in the form of *cordões* – groups that were formed in each neighbourhood and went around dancing with masks, costumes, flags and drums. It was more exciting too, because there were hundreds of groups, rivalling each other. Some were sworn enemies – almost always because one group had taken the other's flag in a dance and had forced them to rescue it from their territory. When the two opposing groups passed each other in the street, there were fights that made stallholders shut up shop – legs flew, daggers were drawn and blood ran down the gutters. The police intervened with their batons and ended up on the receiving end too. But if one group were imprisoned and ran the risk of spending the whole of Carnival in jail, their adversaries grouped in front of the police station and sang for them to be freed. The fact that the party-goers were masked made identification difficult, and there were some who took advantage of this to commit minor acts of cruelty. Even today, in the Carnival of the distant suburbs or the small towns near Rio, the *clóvis* or 'ball-beaters', pranksters with masks and loose clothing, still survive – they are clowns, in fact, which is where the name *clóvis* comes from. Their weapon is a ball (made out of a bladder, rubber or plastic) tied with string, which they use to beat on the ground and frighten children and passers-by.

At the end of the nineteenth century, these anarchic *cordões* turned into *ranchos*, which were more peaceable and organised, and were brought to Rio by the Bahian black Hilário Jovino. In these groups, the clothes and the choreography reproduced tribal processions in Africa. But, as many mulattos and poor white people, women included, joined them, the primitive drumbeat was supplemented by groups of singers and 'erudite' instruments – strings and woodwind. Before this, racial mixture in Rio had mostly happened in bed, between the masters who could do anything they wanted, and the prettier slave-girls. With the *ranchos*, however timidly, this mixture began to worm its way into the music and into the streets. And the *cordões*, which everyone thought had been killed off by the *ranchos*, were reborn in a simplified form as *blocos*. Switching little by little from violence to good-humoured banter, these groups have kept the true, spontaneous, popular flame of Carnival alive.

Already in those early days, Carnival involved the whole population. Whether they approved of it or not, the press and writers gave them ample coverage (there's a huge contemporary literature on nineteenth-century Carnival). Months of preparation culminated in the three or four days of partying. The parades cost money, and the revellers borrowed it from shopkeepers. The latter always made a profit from Carnival, selling devil's costumes, skull masks, conical hats, noses with spec-

tacles on, false breasts, whistles and the instruments
for the *zé-pereiras*. The government itself encouraged the festivities: in every square they provided a
bandstand, each with its own band. When he was a
child, the future Emperor Pedro II let off steam at
the *entrudo*, squirting water at the noble ladies'
décolletages. Afterwards, the formalities of his role
forced him to abandon such pranks; but his heart
still beat discreetly to the rhythm of the drums and
the pans. It's said that, in the palace in Petrópolis, a
boy (who would later become an ambassador during the Republic) threw a handful of confetti, without warning, into his open mouth – and the already
aged Dom Pedro, almost choking, thought it was
funny. And it wasn't even Italian paper confetti, but
little plaster pellets, made here in Brazil.

In 1889 the monarchy was overthrown, the
Republic set up, and with the inevitable acrimony
that follows a change of regime, some of the new
rulers dared to threaten Carnival – and came a
cropper. In 1892, Rio's Prefecture decided that
Carnival should not be celebrated in February because of the heat, which was 'propitious to rain and
fevers', but in June, in the symbolic carioca winter.
The carousers pretended to obey the order and took
the opportunity to have Carnival as always, in
February, as well as the 'official' one, in June, so
Rio had two Carnivals that year. The following year,
the order was rescinded. That was one reason why
the extremely popular Baron of Rio Branco, father of
Brazilian diplomacy, noted with amusement that in

Ruy Castro

Brazil (he meant, in Rio), there are only 'two things that are organised: disorder and Carnival'. In 1912, the Baron unwisely died two days before Carnival, which caused a colossal commotion. National mourning was decreed and Carnival was postponed to April. Once more Rio, much as it loved the Baron, took to the streets in the next few days, then again on the day the Prefect wanted, which coincided with Easter. From then on, the authorities stopped meddling with the date of Carnival.

At the very beginning of the twentieth century, after the Prefect Pereira Passos had knocked down a good part of the old colonial city and turned it into a replica of Paris, Rio and Carnival became 'civilised'. The *entrudo* was completely abolished – instead of water and rotten items, people now threw real confetti and streamers at one another, and sprayed one another using *lança-perfumes* [perfume squirters]: much more agreeable. The new electric trams were turned into floats, and went around loaded with revellers standing on the seats and the running boards. In 1900, Carnival got the first song expressly made for the festivities, the march 'Ó *abre alas*' ['Out of the way, I want to come through'] by the pianist and composer Chiquinha Gonzaga. And chance created a tradition that would go on for years: the motorised cavalcade along the Avenida Central which had been recently inaugurated.

This happened on Carnival Sunday, 1907, when President Afonso Pena's daughters were in a festive mood, being driven along the mile and a half of the new boulevard, from one end to the other and back, in the presidential car. Right away, other people with cars (Rio already had a few hundred cars that year) liked the idea and did the same thing. The line of gleaming model T Fords, with their tops down, decorated with streamers and full of people honking their horns and singing, driving along the avenues carpeted with confetti, would be an attraction of Carnival for decades to come. It was romantic, but it must also have been tense: with so many lads and girls squeezing up against one another on the seats, one can just imagine the rubbing thighs, the wandering hands and the wet knickers – these were the limits of the excitement these young men and women of respectable families were allowed.

But, then again, this was only the white people's Carnival: a belle époque party with corsets, petticoats and starched collars. All sexual excitement and lechery was repressed; it was a Carnival from the navel upwards. In comparison, the blacks from the poor neighbourhoods, who from about 1860 had been stirring an unholy musical brew, were already making a much better Carnival – because it was explicitly from the navel downwards. This was the one that would win out.

It certainly is fascinating that, of all the foreigners who brought their arts and customs to Rio, those who have left the deepest marks on culture – on music, football, religion, food, language, to say nothing of their swing – are the only ones who didn't come of their own accord: the blacks.

In the past, we have to admit sadly, Rio was one of the largest slave markets the world has seen. For centuries, more than two million Africans entered its port, in chains, almost all of them from Guinea, Angola and the Congo, half of these just between 1808 – when when Rio welcomed the Portuguese court – and 1850, when, under British pressure, the slave trade finally ended. Not all the slaves who passed through Rio stayed here. The majority were taken inland, to the coffee plantations or gold mines. But the ones left were enough to make Rio the biggest black city in the world. In 1849, counting both slave and free men and women, carioca blacks were 90,000 in a population of 200,000 – in New Orleans at the same time, there were fewer than 20,000. In the second half of the nineteenth century – because of the end of the trade, high numbers of deaths among the slave population and the massive influx of European immigrants – the city 'whitened' statistically. Not to the point, however, of stopping the progress of a piquant afro-carioca culture that began to flow under the streets cobbled with *pé-de-moleque* – literally, 'urchin's-foot', a name coming from the hardened feet of the (usually) black children that ran over them.

This process was inevitable, because slavery in Rio was different. Even at its zenith, it never fitted the cliché: pictures of silent, sleepless blacks, their eyes burning, at the back of the slave-quarters, stumbling out into the dawn for work, with the foreman's lash already on their backs. That might have been reality over almost all of Brazil, but not here.

To begin with, carioca slaves had, for the most part, urban functions. Some served as domestics, living in the same houses as their masters, and also appearing in the presence of visitors. Others worked outside, and so spent most of their time in the street. Many belonged to foreigners, so that as well as Portuguese, they learnt to speak French, English or Spanish, and became sophisticated cooks. To work as stewards or butlers, they had to learn 'good manners'. When they went out with their masters on formal visits, their feet were bare, but they had to dress up with breeches, frock coats and wigs. Apart from this, carioca slaves, both men and women, were very handsome – as Rio was almost always the first stop and much of the country's wealth was concentrated here, it was natural that the tallest and strongest, with the best teeth and bone-structure, should be bought for keeps. Some had been princes and princesses in Africa. It's not surprising that in the languid intimacy of their large houses, some of the masters couldn't leave these beautiful black women with their naked breasts alone – a reality which their white wives, many of them plain and with more than a hint of moustache, didn't dare question. The children of these liaisons, mulatto and forward, were mostly born free, and were taken into the family; they could climb up the social ladder.

If one discounts the humiliation essential to slavery, the carioca slaves lived much better than their cousins who'd been sent to the plantations. This isn't to say that they didn't get beaten too – their resentful mistresses kept a little whip at the ready for 'trivial' matters, and, if they tried to run away, they were sent to the pillory, where those who did the flogging were paid by the state. But, considering the chances they had to flee, attempts were few. When they did get away, they collected in *quilombos* which sometimes were given legal status, and in a short time they were trading with the whites. One of these communities, in Leblon, which was then a long way from the city centre, cultivated camellias for the city, and you could go there on a (horse-drawn) tram – could anything be more carioca than that?

Life in the street, where they spent a good part of the day, already gave the slaves a feeling of freedom. They did everything, from taking messages and small packages to heavy work like transporting water in huge earthenware jars and carrying pianos on their backs. There were slaves with all kinds of occupations: cobblers, dock-workers, boatmen, fishermen, carpenters; they handled gunpowder, made bricks, rolled cigars, lit streetlamps, swept the streets, sold poultry, tarts, sponge-cake, anything you can think of. There was no shortage of lazy whites – a swarm of well-dressed layabouts – who kept them for that very purpose: to sell their services in the town and give their masters the greater part of what they earned. It was demeaning, but with the money left over, some slaves collected a nest-egg that allowed them to buy their freedom (and straight away, now as ex-slaves, to buy one or two slaves themselves). All right, not everything was as cosy as this – in fact, nothing was very cosy: one of the jobs reserved for the humblest slaves was to tip the barrels of shit produced in the town houses into the sea (the barrels were called 'tigers', because everyone ran away as soon as one of them appeared at the corner of the street). In spite of all this, there were cases of newly freed slaves who went back to Africa, didn't think much of what they saw and took ship back to Rio.

One of the explanations for the fact that carioca blacks have always been sharp, fluent in speech and at ease in any situation – in contrast to whites and blacks from other regions of the country – may lie in their ancestors' familiarity with street life. At loose in the city among poor whites and free blacks, they learnt to look out for themselves, to master the rules and deal with the police – that's how the *malandros*, the city's wide boys, who lived off their wits, came into existence. They also learned to defend their beliefs and traditions. When do you think they came on to the Rio streets, parading in *ranchos*, *blocos* and *cordões*? When slavery was in full swing: it was only completely abolished in 1888. And when abolition came, many of them were no longer slaves, but barbers, tailors, milliners, jewellers, typesetters. Or they had never been slaves, like the ex-typesetter Machado de Assis.

Others were also artists: singers, composers, musicians. For them, the shackles had never meant much – they'd always been free.

Try to imagine it: a mini-Africa embedded in the almost-European Rio of 1900. The heart of this enclave was the Praça Onze de Junho, near to where the Sambodrome now stands. At the turn of the nineteenth and twentieth centuries, that was where the Bahian *tias*, literally 'aunties', were concentrated – a constellation of fat, no-nonsense black women, who, after they had arrived in Rio some years before from Bahia, soon ruled the roost. For practical purposes, even in the eyes of the police, they were professional sweet-makers. They earned their living selling tapioca cakes and coconut sweets in the city Centre, seated on stools on the pavement with their trays and their gleaming white clothes. But they didn't just weave their magic with their sweets. In real life, they were the mistresses of the *candomblé*, the priestesses of African cults, and they had a enormous authority in Rio's black community. In spite of frequent police raids, it was in their houses that the rituals dedicated to the birthdays of the 'saints' – *orixás* [divinities] like Xangô, Nanã, Ogum and others – took place. These ceremonies were followed by parties which lasted for days, with huge feasts, quantities of booze and lots of music.

The most famous of the 'Bahianas' was Auntie Ciata, a mulatta whose influence on Rio's culture could maybe fill encyclopaedias. In the sitting-room of her house on the Praça Onze, Ciata kept an eye on her fifteen children, friends, and guests, and encouraged the *choros* played by, among others, a lad called Pixinguinha on a flute. In the kitchen, she supervised the pans where the food for the crowds of people and the offerings to the gods originated. In the space at the back of the house, Ciata took charge of the ceremonies for the saints, sang, danced, and kept the 'samba' moving. The word samba came from much further back – 1838 at the latest. It didn't describe the rhythm we all would come to know, but any festivity with a dance propelled by clapping, clicks of the tongue, drums and suggestive movements, called *umbigadas* – a rubbing of navels [*umbigos*] between men and women. The word must be a euphemism: if you're not in urgent need of a diet, try and rub your navel against someone else's without rubbing your genitals too.

At a certain point, Ciata's power overflowed the limits of Rio's 'Little Africa' and filtered into the offices of the white world. In 1915, through a minor government employee who took her to the presidential palace, Ciata, with her sorcery, supposedly 'healed' President Wenceslau Brás of a leg-wound which had resisted conventional medicine. Brás was grateful, and in exchange, Ciata asked for her husband to be given a job in the civil service. He went to work as a police clerk, and so Ciata was protected from the unwelcome attentions of the law. This was not to be sniffed at, for historically, the Rio police seemed to have two fixations: persecuting African cults and repressing *capoeira*. This second task was not so easy – not many policemen could stand up to these strong, athletic black men, experts at tripping people up, their feet flying at their enemies' heads (who if pressed, too, might pull a knife). Since they were afraid of the *capoeiras*, the police preferred persecuting *candomblé*. To make it worth their while, they confiscated some guitars and tambourines.

But, some time later, the atmosphere changed. Ciata became so well known that white *demi-mondaines* called on her to buy or rent her 'Bahian' outfits to wear at Carnival balls. Then they were followed by the cultivated girls of Botafogo and Laranjeiras, and soon Ciata was running a profitable clothes business. Also, people of various classes – socialites, politicians, military men – had begun to consult her for her prayers and cures. It's also likely that it was from Ciata's house and those of other 'aunties' like her, that Bahian dishes traditionally reserved for the gods (chicken *xinxim*, *vatapá* and *sarapatel*) emerged, and turned out to suit the tastes of the white carioca élite.

Ciata looked after her reputation, and made friends with journalists. They went to her parties attracted by the music, and their ears pricked up when the drumbeats and chants, enriched by flutes, guitars, ukuleles, and a new, creative percussion, began to show the influence of European melodies and harmonies. It was no coincidence that something similar was happening at the same time in New Orleans, which would end up as jazz. In Rio, it was samba that was about to be born – no longer as a synonym for a festival in the black community, but as a new type of music.

That was all that was needed. For Brazilian music, the appearance of samba opened up new horizons. For Rio, it was as if the city had finally found its voice.

The first samba to be a hit with the word 'samba' printed on the record label, *'Pelo telefone'* ['On the phone'], was composed – where else? – in Auntie Ciata's house. According to several accounts, it was the collective creation of the young black musicians who were always to be found there, amongst whom were Donga, João da Baiana and Heitor dos Prazeres, all of them sons of Bahian 'aunties', but themselves born in Rio. Whether it was composed collectively or not, the one who copyrighted it in the National Library and went down in history as its author was Donga, the guitarist, in partnership with another *habitué* of Ciata's, the white reporter on the *Journal do Brasil* Mauro de Almeida. It's possible that Mauro, whose wonderful nickname was 'Cold-foot Turkey', only gave a final form to the several versions of the lyric that had been sung in Ciata's house, but this doesn't detract from the marvellous fact that the first official samba was signed by a black man and a white man.

Recorded at the end of 1916, '*Pelo telefone*' was sung on the streets in the Carnival of 1917 and it turned out to be brilliantly suited to it: the song was cheerful, cheeky (the people altered the words to make fun of the Chief of Police, no less) and good for dancing to. The word samba became fashionable and entered into usage in the streets and the newspapers. Advertising took it up, and suddenly, samba was everywhere. Some time later Donga saw '*Pelo telefone*' was being played in a theatre in Niterói, where you had to pay to go in. He went to claim his royalties from the owner who, mystified that Donga should want to be paid for his music, called the police to arrest him. They were only too happy to oblige, and so Donga became the first of a long list of Brazilian composers who've been robbed of their royalties.

With the success of '*Pelo telefone*', it was realised that except for the cheery, but now rather ancient '*Abre-alas*' ['Make way for me'], by Chiquinha Gonzaga, Carnival had spent centuries living off the same *lundus*, *modinhas*, waltzes, polkas, quadrilles, *batuques* and *maxixes* that were there all year round. There had never been a type of music specific to the festival itself. Now this music did exist, and it was the samba. Then began the tradition of composing sambas specially for Carnival. The first great composer appeared, the pianist Sinhô, a canny mulatto, and friend of poets and members of high society. In 1920, Sinhô outdid himself: he coupled the traditional polka to new American ragtime (both of them being descendants of European military marches), gave the resultant hybrid the mischief of the Praça Onze, and with 'O pé de anjo' ['Angel's foot'], produced the model *marchinha*, the other great Carnival rhythm – a kind of Brazilian sister of the foxtrot, with which it shared several ancestors.

But the setting was not ready yet. At the end of that decade, the samba, softened by the black composers of the Estácio neighbourhood, among them Ismael Silva, reached its definitive, adult form. With its long phrases, it became more drawn-out, less jumpy, and could be danced at a walking pace, with a soft shoe-shuffle (for the men) and a swing of the hips (for the women). This was a samba that suited carefully composed, romantic and sophisticated lyrics. Many were too sad to be sung at Carnival balls. The *marchinhas* filled that need. The mocking, obscene lyrics, written with a mixture of gauche erudition and carioca slang, were their speciality, and they began to dominate Carnival. With the samba to sing of love and the *marchinhas* to take the mickey out of everything (love included), the city now had the perfect musical backing to let its hair down.

Between 1930 and 1960, in terms of good music and bad behaviour, Rio had Carnivals like there's never been, at any other place or time. Though it is a reasonably Catholic city, it produced, right at the feet of Christ the Redeemer, Carnivals that were more pagan than Egyptian paganism itself, or Roman bacchanals – here, Apis the bull would have been turned into a bar snack and Bacchus wouldn't have got a look-in at the *Clube dos Cafajestes* [Plebs' Club], a brotherhood of well-bred, educated young men who used the general enthusiasm for healthily immoral ends such as dances, parties and orgies, with a fight or two along the way to keep everyone on their toes.

Because it almost always falls in February and coincides with the full splendour of the summer, an invitation to scanty clothing, Rio leaves other, winter Carnivals far behind in enthusiasm, including the ones that inspired it; Nice and Venice for example (they still are what they always were – beautiful masked balls). Carioca Carnival also made one see that in comparison, the New Orleans Mardi Gras was a high-class party, exclusive and racist, in which blacks and whites enjoyed themselves equally, but separately. In Rio, the samba and the *marchinha* put everyone on the same level. Since they appeared, there's only been one Carnival for blacks, whites and mulattos.

Its creators and interpreters were people of every race and class, working and enjoying themselves together. In the thirties, the singer Mário Reis, white and from a rich family, sang the sambas that Ismael Silva, black and poor, composed in partnership with white, middle-class Noel Rosa; he was accompanied by an orchestra whose players were black and white. Of the three greatest singers of the time, Francisco Alves was white, the son of Portuguese parents; Orlando Silva was mulatto, and kept his hair straight by ironing it; and Silvio Caldas, dark-skinned, with his hair in little waves – what was he? He was the 'dear little *caboclo*', which usually refers to someone of Indian and white ancestry. But what did it matter? At the end of a show, in a theatre or a radio station, they left together and sat at the tables of the Café Nice, on the Avenida Rio Branco, or some scruffy place in Estácio, and the samba went on. These mixtures were part of Rio's routine.

To tell the truth, this was nothing new. The carioca military bands at the end of the nineteenth century were mixed, and the most important of them, the Firemen, had a black conductor, Anacleto de Medeiros. And after all, '*Pelo telefone*' had already been signed by both a black man and a white man. The first orchestra for sambas and *choros*, *Os Oito Batutas*, [The Eight Smart Guys], formed by Pixinguinha (the lad who had played the flute at Auntie Ciata's house) in 1922, was half-and-half black and white, four of each, and played for mixed audiences in cinemas and theatres. Some years later, when radio appeared, black players of any instrument were regularly employed on the Rio stations (in other Brazilian cities, they were only allowed as singers or percussionists). The American recording companies with headquarters here were never ham-fisted enough to force their Brazilian branches to produce 'race records' (cheap records with black artists, intended for customers of the same colour), as they did in the United States with jazz-players. Samba and jazz may have been born at the same time, from the same African grandparents, and teethed simultaneously, but their careers were very different. (Isn't it disgraceful, for example, that jazz should have taken twenty years to have its first 'integrated' combination? This was the trio formed by the clarinettist Benny Goodman in 1936, which included the black pianist Teddy Wilson; and, at the start, it was only for studio recordings, unseen by the white audiences.)

Someone once remarked with astonishment that Brazilians are 'black people of every possible colour'. If they were referring to cariocas, who are proud of this mixture, it couldn't be better expressed. Here we are all black and proud of it, from the green-eyed mulattas to 'whites' like me, with coffee and milk in their families. This isn't to forget the real blondes, with fair skin, blue eyes and European surnames – they might have all these things, but as soon as they move their hips and dance the samba, they can't deny their background either. Rio is an exuberant kaleidoscope of skin and eye colours, of hair textures, shapes of nose and lip – the result of five centuries of nooky in hammocks, bunks, *chaises-longues*, four-poster beds, standing up against a banana tree or right there on the beach, with the sand getting in. Everyone in Rio has a foot in Africa, and those that haven't like to say they have. If for no other reason, because they can't swear they haven't. How can we know what massa was doing with granny in the back kitchen in 1850?

In 1930, carioca Carnival started to become an industry, a musical assembly line that directly created thousands of jobs, and thousands of others in their wake, and produced an enormous amount of money. From August or September every year, composers, lyricists, singers and instrumentalists left the romantic songs of the 'middle of the year' behind and flung themselves into producing the sambas and *marchinhas* to be sung at Carnival. For the next five months, the record companies worked non-stop, and Rio's musicians, with more commitments than they could attend to, could eat prawns every day of the week. There was a frantic secret trade in songs: sambas and *marchinhas* were sold under the table in dozens by poorer composers with no access to the singers. Everything revolved around Carnival, even the advertising industry. Other people made money too – the makers of tambourines and *cuícas* (samba can't exist without them) and the kids who went up into the favelas to chase the cats whose skins were used for these instruments. (One day, someone will write about the thousands of cats who gave their lives for Carnival. This massacre lasted for decades, until acrylic came to save them.)

Foreigners wondered: 'All this, just for three or

four days partying?' Of course not. In those thirty years until 1960, Carnival effectively began in November, with the new songs gradually taking over the clubs, streets and houses of Rio, even invading government offices: it would be no surprise to hear a minister humming the latest tune. Through records, films and, more than anything, through radio, these songs spread nationwide as the summer progressed. Their spark was lit in the thousands of pre-Carnival balls, and with Rio as their fuel, they blazed out over the whole country in the four days of the festival. There was no television yet, nor was there any need for it – the echoes of Rio's Carnival spread everywhere. It was said that, during Carnival, the President of the Republic ceded his authority to King Momus, a fat, cheerful personage who presided symbolically over the festivities. And rightly so: with the country at a standstill, there was no one more pointless or useless than the President. King Momus himself, chosen among revellers weighing more than 280 pounds, was important for disseminating the good cheer. Some Momuses kept the job for years and the longest-lasting of all, Nelson Nobre, said that, in the fifties, he lost fifty pounds every Carnival – he had to appear at all the balls, sweating under his tinplate crown and a velvet costume in temperatures which – in the dance halls jammed with people and with no air-conditioning – went beyond 40° centigrade.

Musically, nothing could be more democratic than Rio's Carnival. The same *marchinhas* were played at all the balls – in clubs, hotels and small theatres as well as the gala occasions in the Theatro Municipal (the opera house) and the Copacabana Palace hotel. No one stayed at home, and if they had no invitation to a club, there was free, twenty-four-hours-a-day Carnival in the streets and squares, where everyone mixed in and any old rags could be used as a costume. A white sheet wrapped round you like a toga, a bunch of herbs behind each ear, a pair of sandals, a toilet seat with wire strings for a lyre, and hey presto, you could appear as Nero. How many times has Carnival folklore produced the following story? Two masked dancers got to know one another in the street and danced all night, kissing and embracing. As the day dawned, purple with passion, they took their masks off – and found out they were brother and sister. Still worse, husband and wife. Don't worry, these were exceptions. The rule was torrid encounters between couples unknown to each other, their urges satisfied wherever – against a wall, on the beach or in the back seat of car – and their bodies burning with the collective heat of Carnival.

'Grandmother? How do you expect me to feel like a grandmother?' a friend of mine said to me indignantly the other day. 'In Carnival in 1962, I was twenty and I spent four days dancing, with my arms around someone's neck. Every night I had a different lover. Sometimes more than one, because I went from one ball to another. I cavorted around at the

Theatro Municipal, the Copacabana Palace, at
Quitandinha, Glória, Monte Líbano, and at the
Marimbás. I went through four costumes: an Indian, a Tyrolese milkmaid, a pirate and a cowgirl.
In the daytime, I cleared my head on the beach or
went round with some group or other. I was elected
the best pair of legs in the *Bafo da Onça* [Tiger's
Breath] *bloco*. I had a little fling at the Barra da
Tijuca with an Italian cinema director – I forget his
name – some sand got in, but it was worth it. For a
week, I don't remember sleeping at home. I sniffed
ten tubes of ether. All that and you call me a
grandmother?'

Not many cities can have so many men and
women over sixty who have a clear memory of
the mischief they got up to when they were young.
They've had their fun and have reached advanced
years, as you might say, but they're still active and
cheerful. When you talk to these old-timers, you
won't hear them snarling with frustration at the
permissiveness of young people today. On the contrary, there are some who think that, in the past (the
forties, fifties or sixties), it was worse (or better);
that kind of permissiveness didn't exist in those
days, and they had to invent it. Also, beyond the
craziness, there was an atmosphere of elegance, a
touch of class, which didn't depend on money or
social standing.

Rio's Carnival was an international catwalk and
its most extravagant balls were those in the Theatro
Municipal and the Copacabana Palace, featuring

the members of café society, Hollywood stars and European and American millionaires. But no carioca had to be rich to get in and have fun. Apart from the invitation, all that was needed was a hired tuxedo or a costume – which was basically only important at the door because, by three in the morning, the black ties were undone, jackets and shirts unbuttoned or removed, and the costumes, above all the female ones, reduced to shadows of their former selves. The foreign luminaries, too, were suitably reduced to the level of mere mortals.

It was at the Copacabana Palace, in Carnival 1963, that the playboy Porfirio Rubirosa lost his wife Odile in the middle of the dance floor, to the accompaniment of the old *marchinha* '*Maria escandalosa*' ['Scandalous Maria']. Rubirosa, a veteran of marriages with the millionairesses Flor de Oro Trujillo, Doris Duke and Barbara Hutton, was also envied for certain attributes – in Parisian restaurants, his name was given to those pepper mills that are used for *steak au poivre*. In the middle of the ball, Rubi realised Odile had disappeared. He only discovered her when it was already daylight, 200 yards away, happy as can be in the arms of a local Lothario who'd dragged her to a nightclub in the Praça do Lido. Again, in the Copa in 1965, Romy Schneider, drunk as a skunk and perilously perched on the front of her theatre box, spilled champagne into the open mouths of a group of merrymakers some yards below. That was fine – except that Romy was still identified with the image of the

Empress Sissi, whom she'd played in three choco-late-box movies. Sweet Sissi, then, nearly out of her mind with excitement, was only prevented from jumping down to join the lads by her lover, the Brazilian playboy Jorginho Guinle. It was no co-incidence that the gang, with their mouths open, were singing: '*Me segura que eu vou dar um troço*' ['Stop me, I'm going to have a fit']. And it was at the dance at the Theatro Municipal, in 1958, that Rock Hudson, then thought of as the most masculine of movie stars, almost had to be tied to the table to stop him flinging himself at his carioca security guards. They invented a romance for him with one of the prettiest women in Brazil, the actress Ilka Soares, but it was no good: Rock ended up being photographed wearing a sash with the words 'Carnival Princess' on it, dancing round the room singing that year's *marchinha*, '*Fanzoca de Rádio*' [I'm a Radio Fan'].

For some reason, there was always a *marchinha* that summed up the spirit of the times.

From the thirties to the mid-sixties, more than 15,000 sambas and *marchinhas* were composed, published and recorded – only for Carnival, be it noted; an average of almost 400 new Carnival songs per year. Of these, only a minority were hits. But the ones that did appeal to the public were sung *ad nauseam* and incorporated into Carnival's perma-nent repertory. They became standards of their genres: sambas like '*Agora é cinza*' ['Now it's ashes']

(1934), '*Meu consolo é você*' [You're my consolation'] (1939), '*Ai, que saudades da Amélia*' ['Oh how I miss Amelia'] (1942), '*Lata d'água*' ['Can of water'] (1952); and *marchinhas* such as '*Teu cabelo não nega*' ['Your hair can't deny'] (1932), '*Mamãe eu quero*' ['Mummy I want'] (1937), '*Touradas em Madri*' ['Bullfights in Madrid'] (1938), '*Jardineira*' (1939), '*Aurora*' (1941), '*Alá-lá-ô*' (1941), '*Piada de salão*' ['Drawing room joke'] (1954), '*A lua é dos namorados*' ['The moon is for lovers'] (1961) – the list of *marchinhas* is endless. Samba might be the noble rhythm for Carnival and for the rest of the year, but it was the *marchinhas* that set the temperature for the frolicking. It was a simple recipe: direct, easy-to-learn melodies, a frenetic rhythm to dance up and down to, and short, cheeky lyrics full of *double entendres*.

Nothing could be less politically correct than the *marchinhas*. Their lyrics were 'offensive' to any group you could imagine: blacks, Indians, homosexuals, fat people, bald people, stammerers, adulterers, ugly women, husbands in general, bosses, civil servants – for every one of these types, several crushing *marchinhas* were composed. But they were so funny or absurd that, incredibly, no one seemed to take offence. Other targets were the cost of living, low wages, water shortages, 'progress' and the destruction of historical parts of the city like the Lapa and the Praça Onze. During the Second World War, they got political and poured ridicule on Hitler and the Japanese. Their composers were the cream of Brazilian musicians at the time: Ary Barroso, Noel Rosa, Benedito Lacerda, Ataulfo Alves, Herivelto Martins. Then there were Carnival specialists, the kings of the *marchinhas*, like Lamartine Babo, João de Barro, Nássara, Haroldo Lobo, Wilson Batista, Roberto Martins, Luiz Antônio, Klecius Caldas, João Roberto Kelly. These were intelligent men, blessed with an inexhaustible vein of melody and humour. Thanks to them, cariocas honed their art of criticising everything in fun – and taking the criticism, too.

Such was the extent of the mockery that one *marchinha* of 1951, taking water shortages as its pretext, even sang the praises of Carnival's worst enemy: rain. The lyric said: '*Tomara que chova/ Três dias sem parar*' ('I wish it would rain/Three days without stopping'). Years later, in the summers of 1966 and 1967, nature did exactly that: just before Carnival it unleashed terrifying storms over Rio that flooded streets, destroyed apartment blocks and killed hundreds of people. But the city reacted to the challenge by putting on the wonderful Carnivals of those years. (Something worse had already happened once. In 1918, the Spanish flu, then devastating Europe, killed 15,000 cariocas in a fortnight, out of a population of 1.2 million. Few families escaped at least one death. But when the epidemic was over, Rio had, four months later, in 1919, the biggest Carnival of its history to date.)

Not all the *marchinhas* were 'anti'. They were 'pro', too – only what they were in favour of was a bohemian lifestyle, the heat, vagrancy, not paying your debts, drunkenness, being a lifelong bachelor, and, of course, nudity (there were dozens of songs about Adam and Eve). Two sorts of women always got good treatment: dark-skinned girls and mulattas (nothing against blondes either). A famous *marchinha*, '*Balzaqueana*' (1950), also praised thirty-year-old women, with a reference to Balzac and his novel *La Femme de Trente Ans* of 1834. Another, '*Chiquita bacana*' (1949) mentioned existentialism – just so you can see they weren't as limited as all that. And Rio, with all its problems, was described with admiration and love – many *marchinhas* were simply odes to the city. One of them, '*Cidade maravilhosa*' ['Wonderful city'], a hit in the 1935 Carnival, became Rio de Janeiro's anthem.

'*Cidade maravilhosa*', words and music by André Filho, had been recorded in the same year by Aurora Miranda, Carmen's sister. With an explosive refrain – 'Wonderful city/Full of a thousand delights/Wonderful city/The heart of my country, Brazil' – a sparkling melody and lyrical, gentle words – 'Cradle of samba and of beautiful songs/that live in our souls/You are the altar of our hearts/That happily sing' – it was born a Carnival classic, played at the beginning and end of every ball. In 1960, when Rio lost its status as capital and became the state of Guanabara, it needed a song to be its anthem, and '*Cidade maravilhosa*' was chosen.

And why not? A heroic, pompous anthem, with a

military flavour, would never have been taken seriously by cariocas. It had to be something colourful, elegant and charming, like the city itself. Naturally, non-residents had no obligation to know about this; and still today, many people are ignorant of the choice. This explains the hips that sometimes begin to sway in official ceremonies in which there are people from outside the city, in a homage to a visitor or the unveiling of some monument. When the ceremony's over, a band plays '*Cidade maravilhosa*'. It's not everyone that understands when they hear the opening notes, and the mayor, the town councillors and other officials get up, put their hands on their chests and sing a Carnival *marchinha*.

Monsieur Perretin, a Swiss, came to Rio on business during Carnival 1911. He was the manager of Rhodia, a French chemicals giant, which had invented an air-freshener called Rodo. He wanted to know why this product, a perfume spray which no one in Europe thought remarkable – what in Brazil is called a *lança-perfume* – sold here in vast numbers. From Rio, at the end of every year, there came orders almost equivalent to the factory's whole output. It had been this way for years. What did the cariocas do with so much Rodo? They told him they used it in Carnival. So M. Perretin came to see for himself.

He came, he saw, and nearly had a fit. What did he see? Thousands of cariocas dancing and spraying themselves with the fragrant, freezing mist they manufactured on the banks of the Rhône. He also saw processions of cars on the wide avenues, with people passing one another and exchanging so many squirts of Rodo that the streets were perfumed. And in the club dances, everyone had a bottle to hand. A fortune in foreign exchange went direct to France, happily volatilised in the carioca atmosphere. M. Perretin, unaware of the Brazilian tendency to take up certain fads as if they were going to disappear the next day, could only see the positive side. In the hearing of a Rio journalist, he declared: 'A people that has a Carnival like this is the happiest in the world.' If M. Perretin also saw anyone in a Rodo-induced stupor, there's no record of it.

The carioca Carnival had been introduced to the *lança-perfume* in 1906. The pretty glass bottles, in ten-, thirty- and sixty-gram sizes, and containing a mixture of ether, ethyl chloride and acetic acid, had come to replace the vials with which, in the *entrudo*, people threw filth at each other. As the *lança-perfume* was imported and on the expensive side, what changed was the target of the squirts. Instead of wasting it on any old tramp, men dedicated themselves to hitting the backs, thighs and bare armpits of the girls dressed as odalisques and Hawaiians, making them squeal and shudder – always a good excuse to embrace them and warm them up with a massage on the spot where the spray had landed. If they squirted at another man, then the preferred target was the eyes – running the risk of blinding the victim, if only for a few seconds. An aura of satanic sensuality grew up around the *lança-perfume*. A journalist of the old school, Alberto Faria, captured the essence of it: 'The ethereal tongue of an aromatic asp, creating sudden shudders in the bosom of seductive Cleopatras or chaste Lindoyas.'

The flasks of Rodo then became part of the carnival-goers' survival kit, along with the costume, the confetti, the streamers and, if possible, a dolly bird slung over your shoulder. Also, with the exception of the dolly bird, children over five went to their own balls with this equipment – including the *lança-perfume*, which they used for the same innocent ends, squirting freezing jets of spray on to little girls with painted lips, or trying to blind each other. But the Carnival always came when these lads grew up and crossed the border separating them from adults. That was when they learnt that the *lança-perfume* could also be used to soak your handkerchief, inhale ('take a *prise*') and feel the effects of the ether – a buzzing in the ears, sounds of bells in the distance, a slight sensation of unconsciousness, short-lived hallucinations and the delirious sensation that, for a few seconds, one's heart has stopped and the world has been swallowed in a vacuum.

In the face of the happiness that had so impressed M. Perretin, Rhodia in 1919 set up a factory in Brazil to manufacture *lança-perfumes* right here and spread the happiness even further. Nothing

could have been more fitting, since it was the
carioca Carnival that had given a whole new meaning to a good proportion of the product. In 1927,
they revolutionised the market by launching a metal
tube: the Metal Rodo appeared. A rival firm took
on the production of a glass bottle, labelled
Columbina. Both versions had their pros and cons.
The glass tube allowed you to control the level of
the liquid and keep it for the moment in which a
squirt on to a costume sleeve was a matter of life
and death. A pity it could break for no special
reason, cutting your hands, your feet, and, if you
carried it in your back pocket, your buttocks. The
trouble with the metal was you couldn't see inside it
– right at the moment when you needed it most, you
found it had given its last *prise*. On the other hand,
it was indestructible: with it, you could bump into
other people and be bumped into in your turn,
dance with a woman sitting on your shoulders
and raise Cain in the dance hall. The Metal Rodo
won out. At the time, a reveller who was also a
modernist poet tried to name his son Metal Rodo de
Andrade – but the name wasn't accepted in the
registry office. A few years later, Rhodia launched
the definitive *lança-perfume*: the Rodouro, made of
gilded metal, from which the spray seemed to come
out even colder, and the *prises* affected you more.

Not everyone who sniffed *lança-perfumes* got
away with it. There were some who put their
handkerchief to their noses and fell down flat,
fainting in the middle of the ball, and so had to

go through the humiliation of being dragged to the bathroom with everyone looking, and brought round by friends. Even those who got along with the product couldn't prevent themselves thinking: 'I've come round!' when they 'came back' from a *prise*. And those who sniffed a lot woke up the next day with the feeling that their heads had rolled under the bed. There are stories of hangovers that lasted till Easter Saturday. Technically, it was a narcotic, but at a time – the twenties and thirties – when, in Rio, it was known that there was an élite that used cocaine, morphine and opium, the *lança-perfume* was seen as a recreational, family drug.

Old magazines with reports on Carnival show people dancing around at the balls with their handkerchief to their nose. But in spite of the popularity of the *lança-perfume*, only a minority sniffed it. There was no drug culture like there is today, and most of the revellers preferred more virile pursuits, like seducing the prettiest woman in the room, going with her to a quiet corner of the club and getting down to business. The supervisors kept a discreet eye on the sniffers, but only to make sure they did nothing out of order. In any case, the *lança-perfume* was a legal product, which only seemed to exist in Carnival. And, by the forties and fifties, the city had grown too much for any control to be exerted. A blind eye was turned to anyone who didn't limit its use to Carnival, and if the authentic product couldn't be had, they spent the rest of the year inhaling pure ether or the popular '*cheirinho da Loló*' ['Loló's whiff'], which was ether mixed with chloroform. The doctors knew, however, that like any inhaled solvent, the *lança-perfume* could be addictive, and cause sudden lowered blood pressure, convulsions, cardiac arrest, breathing difficulties, and – in extreme cases – death, with a smile on the lips.

After sixty years' legality and several attempts at banning it, the *lança-perfume* was finally prohibited in Brazil in 1966, by a decree from the military government. It became a 'crime' to manufacture, sell or use them. At the time, a friend of mine, the journalist João Luiz de Albuquerque, couldn't resign himself to this. When he'd emptied the last tube of legally purchased Rodouro, he concluded that Carnival would never be the same again and kept that tube – to this day – in a kind of shrine in his apartment. He also thought seriously of asking for a job at Rhodia (in the press department or anywhere else), just so that he could ransack the firm's files at the dead of night, rob Rodouro's secret formula, and manufacture it at home.

But João Luiz needn't have bothered. Although they were forbidden, there was no lack of *lança-perfumes* at Carnival for those who really wanted them – smuggled in from Argentina and Uruguay, where they were still produced. You just had to avoid advertising yourself at the dances. That's still the way it is; with the difference that the young cariocas of the twenty-first century don't wait for Carnival, and aren't much worried about discretion. If they're short of Ecstasy, ice or acid, they soak a handkerchief with *lança-perfume* and sniff it openly, at any time of the year, at their raves in the Lapa, Botafogo or the Alto da Boa Vista. At least they've had to resort to using handkerchiefs again.

The parade of open-top cars ended in the forties. The trams, on whose running boards the revellers would hang in bunches, stopped running in the sixties. The *marchinhas* too are going, going, gone – no one's composed them for decades (in fact, they are composed, but no one pays any attention and only the old ones are played). The balls in the hotels and clubs still go on, but they've lost creativity and made up for it with spectacular obscenity. Confetti battles? Don't even think about it – confetti and streamers are for children, and even then because their mothers force them to it. Even King Momus recently had to slim, by order of the Mayor. The traditional costumes have disappeared, too – nowadays, if you see Pierrot and Columbine in a clinch in a Rio street during Carnival, you can bet your bottom dollar: it's two Pierrots. But what has really dealt the blow to Carnival, for some time now, has been the sexual revolution.

With all its transgressive euphoria, Carnival depended on a certain atmosphere of innocence for its existence. Of course – without this relative innocence, what would be left to transgress? And innocence was the thing the world most obviously lost from the sixties on. Carnival suddenly became superfluous as a pretext for a spree. Its great attractions, like kisses stolen in the crowd, sweaty sensuality in the dance halls and the streets, hand and flesh meeting above and below the navel, Arab costumes with no underwear, the dances prolonged in apartments in groups of two or four – all of this was chicken feed compared to what the middle class started doing, with no problems and no guilt, all year round. Even nudity lost its shock-value. Who paid any attention to a leg emerging from a sarong, or a pair of breasts glanced in a flash, if you had a million bikinis on the beaches on a summer Sunday? And how daring were the girls at the High Life ball compared to the liberation of a whole generation? Carnival had lost its meaning. It seemed to be the end of a long, beautiful Rio tradition.

Then, when the nostalgia-freaks were looking back at days gone by and sighing, the samba schools took over; and from 1970, they saved Carnival.

When they appeared, nobody could have foreseen the importance they would take on. The first school to take that name, the *Deixa Falar* [Let Me Speak], in Carnival 1929, today would simply be called a *bloco*, or a group: a handful of poor blacks, elegantly dressed, but not all wearing Carnival costumes, that paraded through the streets singing and playing *cuícas*, tambourines and butter cans, taking with them their acquaintances and anyone else that happened along. Why a samba 'school'? Because it had been founded (by Ismael Silva and his friends) near a high school in Estácio, and took the name to look respectable. But the name said what its aim would be in later Carnivals.

Entire communities that had for a long time been organised in *cordões*, *ranchos* and *blocos* began to come down from the favelas. When these three types of group were joined together with other features of previous Carnivals, they became the 'schools' that taught the other ones everything: Mangueira, Portela, Unidos da Tijuca, Salgueiro, Império Serrano and the small, but cheeky, Vizinha Faladeira [Chatty Neighbour]. They incorporated the drums of the *zé-pereiras*, the allegorical floats of the 'great societies', the costumes from the *cordões*, the master of ceremonies and the flag-bearer from the *ranchos*. The wonderful samba composer Bide invented the drums to establish the bass beat and the kettle-drum; another percussionist, Betinho da Portela, invented the *reco-reco*, a small portable washboard; the composer Herivelto Martins introduced the whistle. In 1940, inspired by the grandiloquence of the samba '*Aquarela do Brasil*', by Ary Barroso, which was to become internationally famous as 'Brazil', the composers made an epic out of the *samba-enredo* – literally, a samba with a plot. They put everything together in a single spectacle and went on adding novelties – such as the 'wings', large sections of the school uniformly dressed, like the 'Baianas', a homage to the old Bahian women like Auntie Ciata. Everything revolved round the *enredo*, epic and patriotic, set in Rio or Brazil in colonial or imperial times.

In a short time the schools managed to soften certain prejudices that still afflicted the dancers, notably the idea that they were vagabonds and troublemakers. On the contrary, Carnival showed that they worked hard to prepare the school for the parade, and were very organised – the parade itself, full of pomp and hard-and-fast rules, was the proof. The public authorities soon woke up to the schools' potential and made the parade along the avenue an official event. The press created an annual competition between them, with journalists and writers as judges, and set up money prizes for the winners. In the middle of the parade, each school stopped in front of the reviewing stand and bowed and curtsied to the Mayor. In this way, the schools tamed the violence of the police, who had to submit to a new reality: they could persecute blacks any day of the year – but, in Carnival, it was their job to protect the dancers on the avenue, and prevent the audience, only held back by a rope, from getting in the way of the parade. Even so, the distrust of the police was so strong that, at the beginning, some of the 'Baianas' nearest to the rope were bearded men with wide skirts and a turban, and a knife strapped to their leg – just in case.

In the forties and fifties, the schools were already serious organisations, though they hadn't the power to supplant the vast Carnival of the radio stations, the balls and the *marchinhas*. At the end of the sixties, when this Carnival was finally strangled by changing habits, the schools – who had had nothing to do with this – grew, got the backing of the white middle class, artists and 'celebrities', and became the main attraction.

Since then, they've never stopped growing. Today, they're big business, with Internet sites, all kinds of subsidiary activities and dozens of full-time employees. The biggest, Mangueira, in partnership with state and multinational enterprises, maintains social projects like community crèches, an enviable Olympic village for training athletes, and even schools, which go from basic education to an advanced course in IT. Others are following its example. Almost all of them operate in the favelas where the drug traffic is established, or near them, and this intimacy sometimes has its dangers. Nobody there is exactly innocent or naïve. And perhaps because of this proximity, the social initiatives of the schools mean that many favela kids prefer a Macintosh to an AR-15. Nowadays there are even people from the schools in the federal administration, helping the government with their experience with the poor.

But of course the real *raison d'être* of the samba schools is still the parade, Carnival itself. With this too, they've lost their innocence. Without forgoing their baroque abandon, their plots have modernised. When they gave up the patriotic ballyhoo, they began to deal with contemporary, abstract, or even 'protest' themes. Each school now takes a year to prepare its parade – work lasts from one Carnival to the next. For this to happen, they've had to go professional. In the last thirty years, the schools have unveiled a figure whose power in the hierarchy is as great as that of Steven Spielberg in one of his films: the *Carnavalesco*. He is the general director of the parade – a multimedia creator, with *carte blanche* to dream up whatever he wants. The first of them, Joãosinho Trinta, won this freedom in the seventies with his *enredos* for Beija-Flor, and passed it on to all his successors. Today, if any *Carnavalesco* gets it into his head to launch a float eighty-seven yards long representing ancient Egypt, nobody will stop him, so long as it fits into the plot: in fact, that's exactly what Max Lopes, of Mangueira, did in 2003.

Under the direction of the *Carnavalesco* operate researchers, folklorists, fashion designers, painters, sculptors, choreographers, set designers, milliners, prop managers, and a number of other professionals, alongside the manual workers: seamstresses, painters, carpenters, blacksmiths, solderers, electricians – closeted for months in the sheds where everything is sewn, constructed and mounted. The quantity of cloth, feathers, stones, sequins, beads and glass drops that covers the nearly 4,000 participants in each of the schools can only be weighed in tons, and remember that the costumes often leave room for a lot of bare skin. In the same way, the wood, metal and polystyrene that go to make up the scenarios on the enormous floats can only be calculated in miles.

Like any other assembly line, the schools depend on suppliers, who in turn depend on manufacturers. Imagine keeping the accounts for all this – each item and everyone involved is paid, gets a receipt, and everything has to be audited. That's what you call running a business.

The time has passed when the feathers for the costumes were got by raiding hen-coops and back gardens. Today the schools buy them in thousands, in farms that breed ostriches for slaughter. They've also begun to use recycled material: several have paraded with floats made of bottles and plastic straws, drink-can rings, and other industrial waste – with unbelievable results for anyone who still thinks that kitsch is a sin. The parade itself has changed. In the past, the progress of the school along the avenue was sketched out with a pencil on a piece of wrapping-paper by the 'Director of Harmony', a cross between a choreographer and a stage manager – now it's done on the computer.

To call this a super-production is understating it. It's *Gone with the Wind* multiplied by *Ben-Hur*. To put on this spectacle, in which thousands criss-cross the avenue, dancing between huge floats, each school has eighty minutes, not a second more. What leaves the gringos open-mouthed is that it has to do this without going very fast or very slow, without missing one beat of the drums, without any of the trucks breaking down in the middle of the road, without one hat falling. And what's more impressive: they do all this without a single general rehearsal – in no serious country would anyone take such a risk with a spectacle of this size.

Who pays for so much extravagance? On their own, the internal finances of the schools couldn't afford all this – after all, they are made up of the poorest communities in the city. They get the money from the tickets to the Sambodrome and an allotment from the Rio Prefecture. Sometimes, some schools get business sponsorship. And almost all of them depend on the *bicheiros* [the people who run the illegal gambling game, the *jogo do bicho*]. But the greater part of the money comes from television rights, which, for many years now, have been big business for everyone: on the two nights of the carioca parade, Carnival Sunday and Monday, the country stops to watch it – a hundred million Brazilians spend a sleepless night, glued to their screens.

However thrilling this might be, it doesn't compare to watching the spectacle live at the Sambodrome, in a box next to the arena. Only there, in person, can one appreciate the absurd elegance of the master of ceremonies and the grace of the flag-bearer; the blood running down a hand beating the drums; or the thread of sweat trickling down the statuesque body of a samba dancer, who has nothing on but a tiny triangle of sparkle on her pubic hair.

Now do you understand why putting a samba-school parade on to the street is more complex than hosting a UN summit with a mere 117 heads of state?

OK, it may be the greatest spectacle on earth, but that's what it is, a spectacle. The real Carnival is the one in which people enjoy themselves, and don't just watch others having a good time. That's why the great carioca Carnival doesn't happen in the Sambodrome. It's gone back to other parts of the city, any part of the city, and when it appears suddenly in your street, it takes the whole neighbourhood along with it, including you, your mother, and maybe even your grandmother. This is the Carnival of the bands and the *blocos*, groups whose informality, *joie de vivre* and agility make the schools look as clumsy and thick-skinned as a nationalised industry. If Carnival was a war, the samba schools would be the Roman army, with their chariots, battering-rams and heavy infantry. The *blocos* and the bands would be guerrillas, small groups in which a reveller can appear from behind a lamppost, shout out an order and change the direction of a parade.

It was the bands that took the carioca Carnival back to the streets when there was the risk that it would disappear from them, and the first was the Banda de Ipanema, in 1965. Thirty leading lights from Ipanema met during that Carnival, contracted some musicians from the band of the Marines to play *marchinhas* from the past, and went out in white suits, singing and dancing in the streets of the neighbourhood. A few street corners later, there were already hundreds of people, many of whom had come off the beaches, in their bathing costumes; others, when they looked out of their apartment windows, saw the shindig going on below and came down to join in the fun. In the next few years, the Banda de Ipanema became an institution in Rio and got to the point where 15,000 people followed it through the streets – the equivalent of almost four samba schools. It grew so much, in fact, that many of its founders moved away, because they couldn't find their old friends in the enormous crowd. Others, like the hard core revellers Albino Pinheiro, Ferdy Carneiro, Hugo Bidet and the 'muse' Leila Diniz, had already died, and each of these deaths had seemed such a blow that the survival of the Banda seemed threatened. But the Banda played on, and took on another character: it became a gay parade, in plain clothes or in drag – some of the latter were truly hilarious. It is possible that, in the not-too-remote future, the Banda de Ipanema may fold. But if this does happen, its torch will be taken up by the many bands it inspired and which are still active, in Copacabana, Leme, Leblon, in the Largo do Machado, in several neighbourhoods in the Zona Norte, and in almost every city in Brazil.

The best Carnival in Rio, however, can be found in the *blocos*. It's a tradition going back to 1880 and which, at the beginning of the twentieth century, gave birth to classic *blocos* like the *Bafo da Onça* [Tiger's Breath], the *Cacique de Ramos*

[Ramos Chieftain], the *Bohêmios de Irajá* [Irajá Bohemians] and *Chave de Ouro* [Golden Key] – this one was always persecuted by the police for breaking a religious festival and trying to parade on Ash Wednesday. (There was also the *Bloco do Eu Sozinho* [The *Bloco* of Me Myself], made up of a single citizen who came out every year for more than fifty years, with a sign bearing the name of his one-man association.) Great sambas and dancers began their careers in the traditional *blocos*. Today, some of them aren't active or have disappeared, but, since the eighties, others have arisen which look like they're here to stay: the *Simpatia É Quase Amor* [Liking is Almost Loving], which takes more than 20,000 people round Ipanema in its wake, the *Suvaco do Cristo* [Christ's – the statue's – Armpit], the *Clube do Samba* [Samba Club], the *Bloco de Segunda* [Monday *Bloco*], the *Bip-Bip* [Beep-beep], the *Barbas* [Beard], the *Monobloco* [Monoblock]. Then there are the smaller, more recent ones, each with a funnier or more ridiculous name than the last: *Minerva Assanhada* [Randy Minerva], *Rôla Preguiçosa* [Lazy Prick], *Que Merda é Essa?* [What's This Shit?], *Nem Muda Nem Sai de Cima* [Won't Change, Won't Budge], *Imprensa Que Eu Gamo* [Squeeze Me and I'll Fall in Love], *Meu Bem Volto Já* [Back Soon Love], *Concentra Mas Não Sai* [Gets Together But Can't Get Moving], *Vem Ni Mim Que Sou Facinha* [Harass Me, I'm Willing], the *Bloco das Carmelitas* (a homage to a nun who escaped from the convent every year to enjoy Carnival), *Cachorro Cansado* [Tired Dog] – and hundreds of others, the majority of them in the Zona Norte, far out of sight of the press and the tourists, but where the best traditions of Rio's Carnival are preserved.

The gestation and birth of the *blocos* are a résumé of the carioca lifestyle. Each one is born of a friendship. It begins with half a dozen friends who, during the year, get together to drink and chat in a bar in the city's suburbs or in a stall by the beach, or even to play football. Sometimes they're from the same profession: doctors, lawyers, architects, bank clerks, journalists, PR men, the unemployed; all kinds of people, of every colour – though it is advisable that none of them should be laying any of the others' wives. While they're eating kebabs, drinking draught beer and *caipirinhas*, someone appears with a guitar or a kettle-drum. A samba is composed, then another and another, and they all learn them and sing them. Around Carnival time, they decide to parade together, taking their wives, kids, the maid, the nanny and anyone else who happens along. Other friends join in and bring their friends. To pay for the rental of a yard to rehearse in and repair their drums, they have a whip-round among the shopkeepers in the area and sell the *bloco*'s official T-shirts – almost always drawn by a nationally famous cartoonist who also, strangely enough, is a member of the group. One or two weeks before Carnival, the *bloco* begins to go out into the streets and immediately captures the sympathy, almost the love, of the neighbourhood – anyone can join in and be carried along by the human momentum. During Carnival itself, there are so many *blocos* from each area that they have to come out on alternate days, under the supervision of the traffic police. If they all came out at the same time, the city would go into gridlock.

Unlike the bands, which use wind instruments and only play the old standard Carnival tunes, the *blocos* depend only on drums and vocal cords to sing the sambas and *marchinhas* they themselves compose – and which, since they won't be relayed on radio or television, say what they want about, or against, anyone. They represent the wicked humour, the critical spirit, the mockery, that are the trademarks of the city.

Carnival is the proof that the cariocas' entrepreneurial spirit, when they decide to put it into action, is formidable. Just imagine if they were to put this spirit to the service of something *really* serious, important and constructive. What would happen?

I don't know, and we don't give a damn.

CHAPTER THREE

From a distance, seen from the outside, Londoners are good at taxis, umbrellas, discreet coughs, dogs and class consciousness. They're good at other things too, but nobody would dare challenge them at these. By the same standards, Parisians excel at baguettes, berets, second-hand books, unfiltered cigarettes and bidets. The Romans, in their turn, at mothers, ice cream, ties, the Virgin Mary and riding pillion on Vespas. These skills don't just happen from one day to the next – it takes centuries of practice to reach perfection. Look at the Romans: they've got 2,500 years of experience in mothers, and they're still perfecting it.

What are cariocas good at? After a rigorous self-appraisal, I'd say we're good at bars, flip-flops, beach tennis, *caldinho de feijão* [black bean gravy], and nicknames. If these achievements seem hollow and irrelevant, let me tell you: in the past it was worse. There was a time when cariocas prided themselves on jumping off moving trams, beating anyone at *porrinha* (guessing the number of matchsticks in someone's hand), picking up a samba tune on the spot, getting into the Carnival ball at the Theatro Municipal by climbing in from outside, and knowing the address of a legendary brothel (which never existed) packed with young trainee teachers. Over time, these qualities have either become impracticable or they've lost their meaning, and we've had to get other, more civilised ones.

Before I forget, I'm joking. When they want, cariocas know how to be serious, and have a tradition of determination and competence in many aspects of life. It's just they don't boast about it. And they are very conscious of their limitations. In spite of all its humanist legacy and the many generations of scientists and scholars it has produced, it's improbable that Rio will ever generate a real philosopher – imagine Heidegger in bermudas eating a kebab on the street; or anyone setting fire to themselves to protest against something – no cause is worth so much sacrifice; the more so if it is a day so beautiful that the beach is unavoidable. But in other specialities, less complex or lethal, cariocas have had something to say, and they've said it. Leaving aside the obvious ones, like playing a *cuíca*, drinking coconut milk, and passing the time showing your footballing skills by keeping a tangerine in the air for hours without it falling, here are some others.

Since 1808, when the Prince Regent Dom João founded our Botanical Garden, Rio has had a strong traditions of botanists, naturalists and geologists. At that time, the Portuguese empire had branches all over the world, which meant that the Botanical Garden was graced with exotic cuttings that the Prince ordered from Africa, India and China – from insatiable carnivorous plants that could swallow a whole swarm of grasshoppers, to the most delicate spices and teas. It was so exotic, in fact, that the Englishwoman Maria Graham, when she visited the Garden in 1823, complained that she couldn't see a single Brazilian plant. But, as always happens here, in a short time it would all be Brazilianised, with caladiums, jacarandas, '*comigo-ninguém-pode*' ['no one can touch me', the poisonous tuftroot] and others, thousands of local specimens gathered in the area and incorporated into the collection. Cariocas found their way round this collection and processed it in less time than it would take you to say 'ecobiodiversity' – even the slaves, who were the first black botanists and naturalists on record. Rio attracted scientists from all over the place – distinguished men like William Swainson, Carl Phillip von Martius, Johann Baptist von Spix, Auguste de Saint-Hilaire and Baron Langsdorf – and from their contact with native Brazilians, there arose studies in the area of pharmacopoeia which must have made the fortune of several European laboratories. Since then, the Botanical Garden has become a living laboratory.

You can spend hours and hours there without exhausting its possibilities: 8,000 plant specimens, almost 200 species of birds, and a huge assortment of butterflies, cicadas, crickets, beetles, spiders, toads, lizards, and other creepy-crawlies; hairy, slimy or with hard shells. All this has been labelled and catalogued – not a single dragonfly escapes the observation of the research institutes. It's a festival of nature and of scientific investigation. Ask the European scholars who still wander round its alleyways – and who until a short time ago, as they did so, might have come across a dedicated amateur botanist and ornithologist, a specialist in birdsong: the composer Tom Jobim (what a pity you can no longer listen to the conversations between Jobim and the *sabiá-laranjeira* [the rufous-bellied thrush] as they whistled to each other). The incredible thing is that the Botanical Garden isn't in some distant, country spot miles from the city's limits. Its seventy acres are right in the heart of Rio, ten minutes from Copacabana, providing oxygen for the city's lungs and avenues. And its main entrance is only a few yards away from some of the best restaurants in the city and from a bar essential for combating an excess of oxygen: the Jóia.

The sea is another place where some cariocas are as at home as they are on dry land: these cariocas are divers, people who spend their lives under water, a hundred feet down, almost becoming a part of the local fauna. Rio is one of the five largest cities facing the sea and, according to these people, it's the one that most mistreats it. In the last few decades, these men have watched the sea darken, the shoals diminish, and thousands of microorganisms go in search of deeper waters to survive.

If, today, Guanabara bay has disgracefully polluted areas, and the beaches and ocean islands are in danger, it's not for lack of warning. The divers never tire of condemning the crazy expansion of the city, predatory fishing and the waste from industry, hospitals and homes that spills into the sea. However, the setting is so beautiful that no one seems to listen. When a tanker pisses oil into the bay, the offence is so obvious that society for once wakes up and for a short time feels outraged. But, according to these same people, the greatest criminal is society itself – and the victim is not just the beauty of the city, but its very future. These men are professionals, not mere dilettanti. They know everything about submarine biology and technology, and, if it wasn't for their work in NGOs dedicated to the protection of the environment, the situation would be still worse.

Rio also has a forte in the human sciences and has always produced first-class historians, sociologists, anthropologists and political scientists. Since the fifties, their work done in institutions like the National Museum, the Federal University of Rio de Janeiro, and the IUPERJ (the Research Institute of Rio de Janeiro, maintained by the Cândido Mendes University) has had an international reputation. Many people from these places teach in European and American universities. I don't know how carioca social scientists behave outside their native habitat, but when they are in Rio, there is a healthy difference between them and social scientists in other places: they're not stifled by academic life. They contribute to the press, are invited to debate on TV, and their undeniable erudition doesn't stop some of them sitting on the juries in samba-school competitions, or practising *capoeira*. And when one of them is criticised for 'vulgarisation' in newspaper articles or lowering themselves to appear on television, you can be sure that the critic doesn't come from Rio.

There are other areas in which, while there's no one looking, cariocas work hard. Rio is the largest scientific and technological centre in Brazil, with important research complexes in the areas of health, engineering, biology, petrochemistry and astronomy. In a country that seems to have an allergy to investing in research, it seems that cariocas do little else. It is the biggest producer and exporter of computer programmes in the country, and its plan for fighting AIDS is cited as a model by the World Health Organisation. It also has, and has had for a long time, first-class clinical medicine in almost every speciality; and an impressive reputation in plastic surgery – Ivo Pitanguy is a familiar name all over the world, not just for secretly re-touching the illustrious noses and multiple chins of the jet set, but also for working with his team in Rio's public hospitals, remedying the victims of accidental deformities. He has been called the 'Robin Hood of plastic surgery', for fleecing the rich to operate on the poor for free. It must be true; there are quite a few women in favelas with noses like Sophia Loren's or Raquel Welch's – all the work of Pitanguy.

And, believe it or not, no one flies like cariocas. You just have to look up. In neighbourhoods like Leblon, Gávea and São Conrado, the sky is crammed with people hang-gliding, flying microlights or para-gliding. This goes back a long way too: it was here, on the Campo dos Afonsos, in 1914, that civil and military aviation began in Brazil. Right from the beginning, Rio has produced more pilots than any other Brazilian state, and still exports them to European and Middle Eastern airlines. That's why, every time I get into a plane, I feel happier when I see that the pilot is a carioca, used to the company of gulls and missiles in the sky. Maybe, too, it's because I never flew from Rio to Manaus with a pilot who, in 1965, regularly flew that route: Paulo Sérgio Valle. At that time, Paulo Sérgio was beginning his career, and in his spare time, he wrote lyrics for bossa nova songs. It was just that he found his spare time while he was flying. While the aircraft was flying itself, as they do, Paulo Sérgio wrote the words for the mel-odies that his brother, the composer Marcos Valle, had just composed – some of them were '*Samba de verão*' ['Summer samba'], '*Os grilos*' ['Crickets sing for Ana Maria'], '*O amor é chama*' ['The face I love']. That's why the poetry was so light, airy and lumi-nous: it was written 30,000 feet up. The lyrics and the plane always landed smoothly and safely at their destination.

Before this rhapsody in praise of Rio gets too

serious, I have to confess that I am a fan of the waiters in some of the oldest carioca restaurants. They've been in the job for forty or fifty years – they've inherited the know-how from their predecessors and have got used to dealing with presidents, diplomats and VIPs, as well as a legion of ordinary people. They've seen everything, and nothing bothers them or makes them lose their aplomb. They've heard everything too, while they have silently served their *steak maison* or Leão Veloso soup. I wonder how many love affairs have begun and ended in their presence, how much political scheming has gone on, how many alliances and betrayals have happened within reach of their eyes and ears. Every one of these delightful gentlemen, veterans of the Lamas, the Café Colombo or the Rio-Minho, must have enough material for 200 novels – which will never be written.

In the end, the cariocas' competence is written in the city's history, and they have no need to boast about it – their incompetence, too, and they don't bother to hide it. Of course, Rio isn't unique: any city has its share of successes and failures.

But there's one category where there's no doubt about Rio, and that's its women.

In 1581, three French ships entered Guanabara bay with the intention of sacking Rio, providing it wasn't going to be too much trouble. The city was unprotected – the Governor, Salvador Correa de Sá, had gone out to kill some Indians and taken his men with him. But his wife, Inês de Souza, organised the resistance. She dressed herself and the other women in the men's uniforms and military hats, lit bonfires at night on Santa Luzia beach and directed some pretend defence manoeuvres. The French, seeing this from a distance, thought the city was ready for a fight, turned their ships around and scarpered. Inês was Portuguese, but many of her young recruits, daughters of the first pioneers, were already young cariocas. Four hundred and some years later, last summer, some girls stretched out on the beach at Posto 9, in Ipanema, saw a policeman in shorts and a T-shirt going along the beach on his motorcycle. They must have liked what they saw, because they welcomed him with a chorus of wolf whistles. As is typical in Rio, the whistles spread round the area in waves. The policeman, embarrassed, turned his motorbike round and went away. They didn't want to get rid of him, as their ancestors had done with the French pirates. But the young man wasn't expecting that kind of thing – whichever town he came from, girls didn't whistle at boys there.

In Brazil, carioca women were the first to go into higher education, to work outside the home, to have a salary and a car, to smoke in public, to separate from their husband and instead of immediately going into a convent, think it was a good thing and go on living their lives normally. I'm talking about a considerable number of middle-class women of the beginning of the twentieth century, not of isolated cases that may have happened before, here or there. The carioca woman was also, in the fifties, the first to wear a bikini, put her brother's dress shirt on, knot it over her navel and go to the beach dressed that way on a weekday, weaving her way through streets full of men in ties off to the office. At that time, this was daring enough; more even than going to the beach pregnant in a bikini, as the carioca Leila Diniz did at the end of the sixties, beginning a habit so natural that it was straightaway adopted by conventional women. Long before this, in the forties, carioca women had been the first to rent an apartment and live on their own, not to give a toss about virginity, and, inverting a centuries-old male game, to choose which men were 'for marrying' and which 'for flirting'. Nowadays, naturally, this is all old hat. But I like to think that, when such things were done for the first time, they involved a certain risk, and there were carioca women ready to take it.

One of them was the *maestrina* Chiquinha Gonzaga, and that in a century, the nineteenth, when women still had to do everything little by little.

For Chiquinha, the problem wasn't men, it was marriage. There was a chronic incompatibility between the sacred bonds and her great, true love, which was the piano. When she was twenty-two, in 1869, married and with three small children, she got an ultimatum from her husband, a rich landowner: music or marriage. Faced with his raised finger, Chiquinha didn't hesitate: she chose music. She left home with her case, her piano and her eldest child, who was six years old (the only one that her husband would let her take, because he was a boy). Her own family disinherited her, but the group around the flautist Joaquim Callado, the inventor of the *choro*, welcomed her to their soirées. Soon after, Chiquinha married again, this time to an engineer, and had another son. But there could be no doubt about it – she was made for partying, not for an egg-stained apron. She sent her second husband off to comb monkeys (as we say in Brazil), again took the son from her first marriage and decided to live by the keyboard – which took nerve because, for carioca women in 1877, piano-playing was just a domestic accomplishment, little more than an ornament in the drawing room (and there was a baby grand or an upright in every middle-class household).

Chiquinha became a professional pianist. She wrote whole musicals (music, lyrics and libretti), for the theatres in the Praça Tiradentes. She composed polkas, *choros* and *maxixes* that are still played today – some remind one of Scott Joplin's rags, only they were written twenty years before. One of her classics, if you remember, was 'Ó *abre alas*', the first tune written for Carnival.

And there's no more delicate *choro* than 'Atraente' ['Attractive']. But it was away from the piano that she showed what she was made of. She sold scores in the streets to buy freedom for slaves, and fought both on and off stage for the end of the Monarchy. The Republic came in 1889, but it wasn't long before Chiquinha was disappointed with the marshals who ruled it, and, in 1893 (with a song), she supported the Naval Revolt against the government of Floriano Peixoto. He ordered her arrest, and she only escaped jail because she had influential friends. In 1902, when she returned from a season of concerts in Europe, Chiquinha brought to Rio a young Portuguese, João Batista Lage, whom she introduced as her 'son'. He wasn't, as everyone knew, but they all pretended to believe it. She, at the age of fifty-five, and he, at the age of nineteen, were beginning a love affair which, this time, would prove lasting – for João Batista was a musician too. Meanwhile, Chiquinha was fighting for the creation of an organisation to protect composers' and playwrights' copyright. When it was founded in 1917, she became its first president, and served in it until her death, at the age of eighty-eight, in 1935.

Chiquinha Gonzaga was an exception. Not many women like her appear per century – at least not in the nineteenth. But other women modelled themselves on her, and Chiquinha was one of the sources of inspiration for another astonishing young carioca woman of the belle époque: the cartoonist and, to everyone's surprise, future first lady of Brazil, Nair de Teffé.

Nair was the daughter of a scientist, diplomat and baron of the Empire, who, even when the

Republic came, hadn't lost his title or his prestige. Born in Rio in 1886, she spent her childhood and adolescence in schools run by nuns in Rome, Nice and Paris. With them she learnt to play the piano and sing, but the major talent she demonstrated wasn't in the catechism: she drew caricatures of the nuns. When she came back to Brazil at the age of nineteen, in 1905, she went to live in Petrópolis, the little imperial city forty miles from Rio.

The Republic hadn't changed the status of Petrópolis as a kind of mini-capital of Brazil. It had been Dom Pedro II's summer residence, and now the new presidents followed his example. French and English were almost its official languages, for the diplomatic corps spent six months of the year there, and the upper classes, foreign visitors, politicians, entrepreneurs and the old and new aristocracy displayed themselves in its drawing rooms. They were the perfect cast for the pencil of this young woman, who was cheeky but not malicious, who exaggerated their features without deforming them or causing offence. The men and women she portrayed had enough sense of humour to laugh at their own caricatures, though Nair's presence did make them more self-conscious of their stuffed shirts and plumped-up bottoms – when they saw she was looking, they would covertly shift position. An older friend of Nair, the patroness of the arts Laurinda Santos Lobo, encouraged her to display her talent in the press.

In 1909, with the pseudonym Rian – her name

spelt backwards – Nair became a cartoonist for *Fon-Fon*, the *Revista da Semana* and other carioca magazines. Parisian publishers 'discovered' her and began to fight over her. Her cartoon portraits of European actors and dancers who performed in Rio began to appear also in French magazines like *Le Rire*, *Fémina* and *Fantasio*. It's possible that Nair, alias Rian, was the first female cartoonist to operate on a world scale. In the following years, there were exhibitions of her drawings in Rio and Paris, and she was one of the illustrators of the book *The Beautiful Rio de Janeiro* by Alfred Gray Bell, published in London in 1914. But this career would be abandoned because, a few months earlier, Nair had taken a step that would leave her no time for drawing. In December 1913, at the age of twenty-seven, she had married Marshal Hermes da Fonseca, who was fifty-eight years old, a widower, frail, almost ready for the embalmer. And, since Hermes was President of the Republic, Nair had become Brazil's first lady.

Why had Nair taken this step? It wasn't for power – she was more than used to the company of powerful people in Petrópolis and Rio (and Hermes, who had been elected in 1910, only had one year left of his mandate). Nor was it for the money – her father, the Baron of Teffé, was rich; Hermes was poor, lived off his presidential salary, and the presidential palace itself had no credit in the neighbourhood shops. It can't have been because of the Marshal's personal charms – he was from Rio

Grande do Sul, Brazil's southernmost state, a nice guy, but with a reputation as a humdrum provincial, whose idea of intellectual activity was horse riding, and, what was worse, with a terrible reputation for being jinxed. Why, then, had Nair married him?

They had met in Petrópolis and started to go riding together. There was friendship on both sides, but not the least notion of a proposal in the air. If Nair had been in search of a fiancé, you'd have thought she'd have plumped for Rasputin before dry-as-dust Hermes. On one of these rides through the woods of Petrópolis, he surprised her with a lukewarm offer of marriage. Nair delicately refused him and later, at home, laughed as she told her family the story. Even so, her father, an old friend of the Marshal, exploded with such extraordinary, excessive indignation, forbidding her even to *think* about it, that Nair, to challenge this unreasonable display of authority, decided to accept the proposal. It was as simple as that – she wanted to show she was mistress of her own destiny. And the campaign against it, making fun of the idea of a marriage between an active, rebellious woman and a man thirty-one years her senior, only made her more determined. Nair put Rian to rest, married the Marshal-President and the two of them went to live in the Catete Palace.

Nair de Teffé turned out to be the most devoted wife Hermes da Fonseca could have found. When he finished his daily presidential obligations and went to the residential wing of the Palace, she took his boots off and brought him his slippers and an eggnog. But, twice in the early days, the impish shadow of Rian came to the surface and interfered with the first lady's composure. The first time was when she interrupted one of Hermes's meetings with the Cabinet, to show the ministers the caricatures she had done of them, printed on her white dress. Grey beards bristled, monocles dropped, purple veins stood out on pink bald pates. The President might have been discussing the Great War, which had just broken out in Europe, and its inevitable effects on Brazil, when his boisterous wife came into the Cabinet room and, with a mischievous air, opened up her dress like a fan to show off her scribblings. That was the ill-humoured way the opposition commented on Nair/Rian's playfulness – Hermes, and ordinary people, loved it. But it was her second exploit at the Palace, on 26 October 1914, that entered the history books: the Night of the '*Corta-Jaca*'.

That year, while in Europe whole nations were exchanging their dress coats for uniforms and marching against each other, the drawing rooms of the Brazilian élite, not realising that the belle époque was over, were still ruled by strict codes of behaviour. Among other rules, at their dances only waltzes, mazurkas and operettas sung in German, Italian or French were allowed; nothing in Portuguese. *Maxixes*, *batucadas* and the nascent samba were thought of as barbarian – belonging to blacks, rogues and vagabonds – and, as such, tolerated, but in their appropriate setting. But for 'appropriate setting' read everywhere that wasn't official – for many members of the Brazilian élite were already falling for these tunes, though timidly. (After all, what were Carnival, the lowly dance halls and the houses of the Bahian 'aunties', but manifestations of this barbarity?) This is the only explanation for the fact that, in a presidential reception for the diplomatic corps and carioca society, the Brazilian first lady included in the musical programme, between one piece by Liszt and another, nothing less than Chiquinha Gonzaga's '*Corta-Jaca*'.

'*Corta-Jaca*' [the title literally means 'cut the jackfruit', the name of a large spiny fruit with sweet flesh] was not the latest hit. It had been composed by Chiquinha Gonzaga in 1895 for a musical revue in a theatre in the Praça Tiradentes, and had re-surfaced since in other revues. It had been given different lyrics, all of them exploiting an improbable similarity between the fruit and a vagina. The most obscene said: 'I'm the jackfruit, very milky / very tasty / good to cut into / I'm the delicious jackfruit / which lovingly/ awaits the knife / to cut it. / Oh, it's good to cut the jackfruit / yes, my love, attack it / yes, yes, that's the way / cut it all over / oh, oh, it's good to cut the jackfruit / oh yes, my love, attack /don't stop.' That night, in the Catete Palace, for an audience of pearl necklaces and be-medalled lapels, this song was performed on the guitar by Nair de Teffé – more Rian than ever.

To be fair, it should be said that Nair didn't sing it. She only played the guitar part, in an arrangement written for her by Chiquinha herself (who was ill, and couldn't come to the Catete). There's no record of the guests, among whom there were professional singers and conductors, having had fainting fits. These only happened some days later, and were the work of Hermes's enemies in Congress. Principally, the crabbed little senator from Bahia, Rui Barbosa, who, thinking the '*Corta-Jaca*' was a dance, roared from the tribune: 'It is the lowest, most coarse, most vulgar of all savage dances, the twin sister of the *batuque*, of the *cateretê* and the samba. But, in presidential receptions, the "*Corta-Jaca*" is played with all the honours given to Wagner's music: and you think the conscience of this country should remain unmoved!'

The old senator wasn't entirely wrong. '*Corta-Jaca*' was a *maxixe*. And the *maxixe*, as well as a rhythm, was a black carioca dance – really shameless, and much in fashion in Europe. Called the *tango brésilien*, it had just been excommunicated by the Archbishop of Paris. It was just that, in the Catete, contrary to what had been said, no one danced to the accompaniment of the '*Corta-Jaca*'. The audience confined themselves to listening, minding their manners. The excitement would have been much greater if they had played Wagner. Not even the Palace chandeliers would have realised what had happened if it hadn't been for the rumpus created by the politicians.

It doesn't matter. With '*Corta-Jaca*', the Brazilian music of the blacks and the poor – low, coarse and vulgar – had finally entered the palaces and drawing rooms. It would never leave them again.

Nair de Teffé and Chiquinha Gonzaga never met, but together they went down in history for having broken Brazilian social protocol. In 1914 this could only have happened in Rio: here, the *crème de la crème* – who determined what protocol should be – rubbed shoulders with the people who could break it. For the same reason, it's not surprising that it should have been two women who did it. Not just that, but women of different colour. Nair was blonde with blue eyes, descended from an English family (Dodsworth) on her mother's side and German (von Hovnholtz) on her father's. Chiquinha was mulatta, the daughter of a black freedwoman and a well-off white man, an army officer, nephew of the military hero the Duke of Caxias, and with doctors in the family. It was natural and very carioca that this should have been the way of it.

As much as or more than blacks, immigrants and mulattos, women starred in some fascinating revolutions in Rio between 1830 and 1930. While, in the provinces, the average Brazilian woman was condemned to use veils and spend the day at home praying, cariocas were used to going out to look in shop windows, having their dresses made by a professional dressmaker, going to the theatre, sitting in tea shops drinking tea or eating an ice cream, lunching or dining out and being brought back home by a gentleman. They also took advantage of these hundred years to create a women's press, take part in republican causes, write erotic poetry, infiltrate the 'male' professions, found feminist associations and fight for the right to vote – which they got in 1932, four years after their British sisters and thirteen years before the French, Italians and Japanese. They were the first to go out in the street in long trousers, backless and strapless dresses, the latter called '*tomara-que-caia*' ['oh-let's-hope-it-falls']. But they only got there after their grandmothers and great-grandmothers had borne a long sentence – more than 200 years – of confinement and oppression.

It's possible that, in the Rio of the end of the sixteenth century, when the pioneer white families were still setting up house on the Castelo hill, women had relative freedom within the walls of the city. When it came down from the hill and spread out, in the seventeenth and eighteenth centuries, they began to be restricted and ended up being shut inside their houses, with access, if they were lucky, via the window. This was not unique to Brazil – even in Europe, the majority of women lived in the kitchen and the bedroom, called their husband 'master' and never appeared if visitors came to the house. What was abnormal here was the severity of this confinement, which lasted until the beginning of the nineteenth century. Women, if possible, were kept illiterate (so as not to read romantic novels or correspond with strangers). They only came out in the street to go to church covered in black mantillas and accompanied by a chaperone. They didn't even have decent windows to look out of, while playing with their hair and taking in the latest fashions.

The windows were blocked by shutters made of thin criss-crossed slats of wood, the famous *gelosias*, that an outsider could barely see through. It was said that the *gelosias* were a precaution against possible attacks on the Governor or the Viceroy when they passed in the street, but everyone knew that wasn't the reason for them. It was fathers and husbands who imposed this law – a backward Portuguese custom, inherited from the Moors, to prevent their daughters and wives being seen from the window by someone with a better offer. What they did manage to do, with this harem mentality, was to make it almost impossible to breathe inside the house, and sharpen women's appetite for going out into the world.

When the port of Rio was opened to foreign trade in 1808, the foreigners who began to arrive here in droves soon realised two things. First, that there were only a few Brazilian women in the streets, and lots at the windows, hidden by the *gelosias*. Second, that though they were hidden, you could see they had beautiful eyes and enjoyed flirting. A typical colonial scene; but Rio was no longer a colony. It had just been promoted, and was now the capital of the kingdom, and had to undergo a complete makeover to correspond to its new status – for the first time in history, a colonial city became the capital of the Empire it belonged to. In a first attempt at cleaning up the city, the *Intendente* Paulo Fernandes Viana (a cross between Mayor, Chief of Police and Head Sanitary Inspector) ordered the destruction of the *gelosias*, which stopped the air circulating, made the houses stink and disfigured the streets. When they realised what this meant, some heads of family resisted the modernisation and kept the *gelosias*. The women, however, got their revenge.

To start a good illicit affair, all that was needed was an exchange of looks through the lattice-work or on the way back from church. From the accounts of foreign travellers, there were many cases of dereliction of duty, with even the most spotless of ladies receiving lovers muffled in cloaks or wearing top hats, who climbed over verandas and found their way into houses with all the skill of Scaramouche. They counted on the complicity of go-betweens, who were the chaperones, maids or ladies-in-waiting of these women. My favourite scene in this line (and the one I like best in the whole vast gallery of pictures of Rio) is an engraving by the Bavarian Johann Moritz Rugendas, of about 1822, showing exactly this: the well-dressed young man has just jumped on to the veranda, where a young, pretty woman awaits him, while the maid, with a roguish look, is just about to retire, or, who knows, go to get the bed ready.

As the years went by, the *gelosias* fell one by one, like little Bastilles, defeated by progress and by the transformations the city underwent. When the final ones were destroyed, the sun came in the windows, and the last carioca prisoners casually plumped up their hair in the mirror and triumphantly went out into the street.

Rio was ready for them.

It may be a cliché, but it's no less true for that: great cities can be masculine or feminine. I'm not talking about the greater or lesser number of each sex to be found in this or that town, but a certain spirit which seems to predominate in some, and not in others. London, New York and Tokyo, for example, are masculine cities – grave, impersonal, no nonsense. Paris, Rome and Rio are feminine – romantic, changeable, seductive. If you've done a bit of travelling, you know that's the way it is.

Masculine cities were born to do business, which is why they are richer and more powerful. If they sneeze, the world might well catch cold – maybe that's why, not long ago, their citizens still wore galoshes. In feminine cities, on the other hand, time spent in search of pleasure prevents them from producing much money – their men and women spend hours sitting in cafés, strolling round the streets, or stretched out on the beach. Though it might not seem like it, these activities at least keep the economy going at a basic level – the moment always comes when you have to pay for some product, even if it's only a bottle of water, some chewing gum or a lollipop. But has anyone counted the number of hours per year that men in feminine cities spend turning their heads to catch a furtive look at the *derrière* of a woman who's just passed by?

This is a practice which, with a greater or lesser degree of furtiveness, cariocas have turned into an art. And, like all the best art, it's free: to enjoy a pair of hips in action (and go on one's way, without inviting the woman for a drink or a trip to a motel) is an act that doesn't enter any production chain, doesn't generate a cent. It really is art for art's sake. On the other hand, it does make everyone's day for a few minutes: the man's, because of what he's seen; and the woman's, because she knows she's been seen; and the whole city's, because it's the setting of this gesture that makes two people happier. For cities of a feminine temperament, that's enough.

Masculine cities tend to be tense and puritan. Feminine cities are relaxed and libertarian. These differences may have to do with the climate, religion, food and even with the stereotypes (doubtless mistaken) that associate men with work and women with play. But that there are cities made for men and others for women, I have not the least doubt – what woman can be successful in New York if she doesn't put on a suit, wear a frown, and prove she's as efficient as a man? (Luckily for her, this is not difficult.) In Rio, this demand is rarely

made, because carioca men don't trouble themselves to fit into superhuman standards of effi-
ciency. Another significant difference is that
masculine cities have those snobbish, exclusively
masculine clubs, where no woman has set foot for
150 years. In feminine cities, such clubs don't exist –
no man would join.

That's why, when you try to represent Paris,
Rome or Rio visually, the cliché of a provocative
female image is almost inevitable. Marianne, the
woman with a Phrygian cap and her breasts bare,
is the symbol of Paris as well as of the French
Republic. Rome's symbol is a she-wolf with teats
full of milk. And there are the symbols of Rio.
Almost every week, some advertisement, drawing
or photo of the city exploits its physical outline,
associating it with a woman: the curves of the
Sugar Loaf and the Morro da Urca next to it
remind one of a slim waist and the shape of the
hips; the Morro Dois Irmãos becomes a pair of
breasts; the lights along Copacabana beach sug-
gest a pearl necklace. You could do an outline of
Rio writing the word: 'Amor', with the 'A' being
the Sugar Loaf. And so on.

Well, I did say it was a cliché.

And to think that, indirectly, Rio owes this to a man
without the least sense of humour, and who never
came our way: Napoleon. In 1808, in an attempt to
hit at England, he pointed his cannons at Lisbon, an
old strategic ally of the English. Incapable of reply-

ing in kind or even resisting, the Portuguese court took ship and hurriedly fled to Rio, taking all they could carry, including the crown and the throne. They were escorted by the British navy, putting the seal on a decision that England had dreamt of for a long time: the opening of the Brazilian ports, so that she could trade directly with the colony. The ports did open, then, and the red carpets were laid out for England in the carioca customs-house. Not even Portugal, which after all owned the place, had as many advantages and concessions in its Brazilian trade.

In no time, the British had taken Rio over: sailors, industrialists, merchants, mining experts, farmers, diplomats, painters, artisans, writers, missionaries, adventurers. What gave life to the dreams of these men, and made them come to face the midday sun? It wasn't just to get rich or save souls. Some of them must still have believed in stories of naked Indians, others maybe wanted to find themselves in the depths of the jungle, still others maybe just wanted to escape from the wife. Whatever the truth, Rio became the busiest port of the hemisphere, with English ships unloading people, and the goods they bought and sold. In 1808, ninety ships entered. In 1810, there were already 422. Sometimes, somebody would make the odd mistake: one Englishman brought woollen clothes, snowshoes and heaters – and managed to sell them all. The majority settled in so well they never went back to Europe. There were so many English people here that in a few years they built a cemetery just for themselves, in Gamboa, so as not to go through the embarrassment of being buried next to Catholics, blacks and natives.

For almost the next hundred years, they dominated the city's transport, rubbish collection, sewers, street lighting and telegraphy, as well as the textile and heavy goods industries, and a large part of the wholesale and import business. At first, their offices and shops were concentrated in the Rua do Ouvidor, a long, narrow alleyway running at right angles to the city's main thoroughfare, the Rua Direita, later Primeiro de Março. But the British didn't have Rio to themselves for very long. From 1810 onwards, many anti-Bonapartist French also began to settle here, with the blessing of the Portuguese crown. Among them were rich men who started coffee plantations in the hills of Tijuca and built beautiful houses there. In 1815, with Napoleon's defeat at Waterloo and the return of the Bourbons to Versailles, it was the exiled Bonapartists' turn to come. Though they were political enemies, the two sides learnt to live together in Rio, and if there were moments when they slapped each other's cheeks and took to their rapiers, a woman must have been at the bottom of it.

With Portugal and France back together on good terms, as he'd always wanted, Dom João placed an order with Paris for an artistic mission – people who would be willing to live here and put

some polish on the new court. There arrived painters, musicians, skilled craftsmen and an architect;
some of them had reputations in Paris. In their
wake came many others, of their own accord.
Suddenly, the French presence looked like an invasion, like the ones the pirates had attempted in
days gone by – except that, this time, they came
without cannon, catapults and muskets. In place of
these instruments of war, the new French were
armed with much more delicate things: tailor's
chalk, tape measures, combs, wigs, thread, pins,
scissors, cosmetics, fans, silks, pompoms, frou-
frous and tutus. From all this, it can be seen that
the difference lay in the human make-up of the two
groups: unlike the British immigrants, who were
mostly grave, mature men – I imagine them all to
have looked like the veteran actor C. Aubrey Smith
– the majority of the Frenchmen who landed here
were . . . women.

The first were the artists' wives and their *femmes
de chambre*. Then came the dressmakers, milliners,
hairdressers, florists, sellers of perfumes or liqueurs.
And a little later, the actresses, dancers and
cocottes. It's possible that many of them, even those
who set up here as professionals with combs or
scissors, had engaged in prostitution in some form
in France. When they decided to set sail for the New
World, Rio must have seemed an Eldorado: a
jungle, free of any refinement and full of riches
ripe for the plucking. They themselves were already
well plucked; their age, and nights spent in Paris or

Marseilles had seen to that. Rio might be their second and last chance in life. Some brought their husbands or current companions.

The fact that they turned to other activities to make a living didn't mean that the Frenchwomen weren't competent at their jobs. The first successfully to install a dressmaker's studio on the Rua do Ouvidor – until then solidly English territory, with its shops for beer, lead shot, gunpowder, bronze beds, ovens and ships' anchors – was Mademoiselle Josephine, in 1821. In a few months, her friends had established themselves there too. In 1822, with their *bonjours* and their *mon chouchoux*, the French had dislodged the majority of the English shopkeepers – who moved, in fury, to nearby, wider streets – and transformed the Rua do Ouvidor into a Parisian *arrondissement*.

In what had been an old side street with grocers' stores and trade in heavy goods, they opened glittering clothes shops, coiffeurs, milliners, shops for gloves and perfumes, and florists, with windows whose mirrors and curtains competed with each other in brilliance and colour. Because of these Frenchwomen, Rio began to discover itself as a vain, feminine city. And it was on the Ouvidor that they awoke carioca women to the possibilities of their new freedom.

The French were the best teachers that these women could have dreamt of having when they came out into the street – and they taught good and bad habits. Until they came, women in Rio made their own clothes with the help of their slaves and used patterns from the time of the discoveries. Now they had people who would do it for them – the dressmakers – and who followed the latest dictates from Paris. To be dressed by a modiste became *de rigueur* in the new court-city, and for this purpose, the carioca had to leave her house, take a cabriolet and head for the Rua do Ouvidor. As she was undressing for the fittings, and being subjected to pins and needles, she breathed in the liberal ways of these women who were, compared to her, 'modern', cosmopolitan, readers of the recent (1782) scandalous novel by Choderlos de Laclos, *Les Liaisons Dangereuses*, and it was as if they had stepped out of its pages.

It was Frenchwomen who taught cariocas to dress, do their hair, put on make-up and perfume, cook, use cutlery, spread their napkin on their lap and exchange imperceptible caresses with a man at the dinner table under the tablecloth. They taught them how to talk, not necessarily the *parlez-vous* – which many cariocas already spoke, though sometimes they didn't know how to read or write in Portuguese – but the art of social conversation, of pleasantries and dalliance. While they were at it, they imparted one or two truths about men, an area in which they had sheets and sheets of experience.

Just as they had done in France, the majority of the dressmakers on the Ouvidor took in outside work in more senses than one – that is, they benefited from the 'protection' of reputable gentlemen of the court. One of them, Madame Saisset, was the favourite of the young Emperor Dom Pedro I, who frequented the back room of her atelier with the amiable consent of Monsieur Saisset. The proof that there was no cause to be upset is the fact that the Saissets were happy ever after, and the son she had by Dom Pedro was left a bequest in the Emperor's will. Madame Saisset must have been an extremely faithful and exclusive mistress of Dom Pedro, but the rule on the Ouvidor was that the discreet courtesans, who allowed themselves to be 'assisted' by older gentlemen, gave themselves for love to attractive penniless young men. This practice is common in that kind of world, but here it had a huge importance – because, by this means, the Frenchwomen also taught young carioca men the sexual ropes.

Yes – because, until then, who could these lads have had a sexual life with? The Indians, who had been such a success just after the discovery, no longer existed – the coastal tribes had been exterminated or 'catechised' since the eighteenth century. There were the slaves, some of them very beautiful, but distant and passive in the face of the young master. The prostitutes of the port area, coarse and toothless, belonged to the sailors and dock-workers. And the young ladies, the 'marriageable' girls, emerged from their domestic prisons and went straight to the altar, and from there to the marriage bed – they had no chutzpah at all. But with the French courtesans, who were gener-

Ruy Castro

ous, experienced, and comparatively amoral, it was different: these lads were faced for the first time with women who were 'superior' to them – not just with a *savoir-faire* in techniques and variations they were unaware of, but also with pride and independence. One of the origins of the historically elastic carioca morals may lie in this élite of young men and women who lived alongside these Frenchwomen at the beginning of the nineteenth century.

This isn't to say that all the Frenchwomen in Rio were temptresses and *femmes fatales*. Daily, there arrived here families of several kinds, from rich people opposed to the Bourbons, accompanied by their servants, to common tradespeople and artisans. It seemed that they inevitably made their way to the Rua do Ouvidor. In the wake of the shops opened by their fellow countrywomen, they set themselves up in other departments of the fashionable retail trade – they were jewellers, clock-makers, tailors, *pâtissiers*, bakers, carpet-sellers, *marchands de tableaux*, booksellers, publishers. With time, they turned the Ouvidor and the area round it into a tropical equivalent of the Rue Vivienne, then the centre of fashion in Paris. They established, after 1830, the first 'international' restaurants in Rio, with a small orchestra of violins, and the confectioneries where, after 1834, a carioca could eat a (vanilla) ice cream, with ice brought from the United States, or a fruit juice (*pitanga*, star-fruit, cashew-fruit, mango or

142

pineapple). From then on, any novelty from abroad appeared here straight away. In March 1839, the first photographs (daguerreotypes) appeared in France. That same year, in December, photography arrived in Rio. Very soon there were carioca women being photographed, apparently with no fear that the photo would rob them of their soul.

The Rua do Ouvidor was where it was at. It was where young women met men of doubtful reputation, witty and amusing – lawyers, poets, journalists, bohemians, idlers – people who, a short time before, had been as remote to them as a *curupira* or a *saci-pererê*, two bogeymen of Brazilian folklore. They took over every square inch of the pavement of the Ouvidor, and it was as if they were occupying several square miles of the country as a whole. Reflecting a reality of the time, the novelists and columnists of the middle of the nineteenth century delighted in taking their female characters for a walk along the street, calling the shops by their real names. The most famous Brazilian writer of the time, José de Alencar, used this ploy more than once in his novel *Lucíola*, of 1861 (in which there is also an orgy scene involving three couples, fixed one afternoon in the Ouvidor and which takes place that same night in a house in the suburbs). Another writer, the German Carl von Koseritz, coined a saying which would be much repeated: 'Rio de Janeiro is Brazil, and the Rua do Ouvidor is Rio de Janeiro.' He hit the bullseye: that was where

Brazil's morals were manufactured. The disparity was so great that, when the Patek-Philippes chimed five o'clock in the Rua do Ouvidor, it was still 1701 in most of the country.

None of this would have been possible if these Frenchwomen hadn't dragged carioca women out of their holes and taught them the delights of danger. In the space of a few years, Rio, obviously Portuguese and African, had also become French. English, too, because, running the essential services, the Anglo-Saxons kept a discreet presence in the city. They hadn't even abandoned the Ouvidor completely: since 1822, Clarks, which furnished shoes for the Imperial household, had been there; Wallerstein's with its shawls and silks, from 1834; and Crashley's, where in 1872 you could buy tobacco, pipes and canes, as well as magazines like *Strand* and *Punch*. Everyone was there: the first street-vendor who appeared there, in 1853, with all the tricks of the trade, was an American called Whitemore, selling an 'anti-foetid' elixir against bad breath. Then there were Germans, Swiss, Spaniards, Italians; all had shops in the area. Many already felt themselves cariocas or were on the way to becoming so, by their marriages with locals, and the children they had by them.

Not bad for a city that, against its own nature, had spent 200 years before 1808 shut up like a clam. Rio was now a part of the world. Finally free to go out in public, carioca women were at home in the city – and, in the years that followed, they would turn the cafés, bars, beaches, and offices (anywhere where their legs could take them, in fact) into their own.

One day, those legs would take them to Ipanema.

Ozzy Osbourne saw red and went to complain to the neighbour who spent the whole day playing a record of 'The Girl from Ipanema', with João and Astrud Gilberto and Stan Getz. Ozzy was right to complain: the beauty of the melody, which seems to be walking along the sand, the rhythmic lightness of the bossa nova and the tenderness of that interpretation must have been unbearable to the riddled eardrums of the old rock-star.

This happened in an episode of *The Osbournes*, a very successful reality show on MTV in 2002. It so happens that 'The Girl from Ipanema', née '*Garota de Ipanema*' is from 1962. It was about time Ozzy and all the Osbournes had got used to it.

During those forty-odd years the tall, tanned, young, lovely girl, created by Tom Jobim and Vinicius de Moraes, hasn't stayed put on Ipanema beach. Her swaying hips have crossed the oceans and caused a ripple-effect in every continent, which her authors had never dreamt of. Since the disc that revealed her to the world (the LP *Getz/Gilberto*, published by Verve at the end of 1963, from which a million-selling single was taken), '*Garota de Ipanema*' has never stopped.

It has become synonymous with bossa nova and has survived the worst ordeals a song can undergo. There's no format, respectable or not, in which it hasn't been recorded: symphony orchestra, solo piano, string quartet, big band, jazz sextet, dance-hall orchestra, lounge and space-age groups, mariachis, a hundred mouth organs, a music float, a *caipira* duo [a form of Brazilian country music], and hip-hop, funk, grunge, acid jazz and new bossa bands. Just when you think it's dead, it comes back to life like Snow White. Its singer-interpreters go from Frank Sinatra (whose 1967 LP established it definitively) to the rapper Floyd the Barber – which gives some idea of what it means from infinity to nought – not counting the bootleg, humorous and pornographic ones. All it needs is to be recorded by George W. Bush.

The main search engines on the Internet each have at least 40,000 pages on 'The Girl from Ipanema'. It would take a lifetime or two to go through it all. Many are about the *jeune fille d'Ipanema*, the *ragazza di Ipanema*, and the *chica de Ipanema*, as you'd expect, but there are pages too in Russian, Greek, Japanese, Chinese, Korean, Arabic and other languages for which the computer would have to have its guts adapted. The score with Jobim's melody, Vinicius's original lyric and Norman Gimbel's English version is available *ad nauseam* on the Net, often with audio. With Vinicius's lyric, there are phonetic transcriptions for gringos who want to sing it in Portuguese, with results like

this: '*Aw-lyuh kee koey-suh mah-izh leenduh /
Mah-izh shay-ya dee grah-suh . . .*'

Americans who know Portuguese and study the
bossa nova quarrel with Gimbel's lyric, comparing
it with Vinicius's and inevitably concluding that the
original is better. They can't resign themselves to
Gimbel having changed the story. In the English
version, the girl passes in the street, everyone ad-
miringly says: 'Aaah . . .', and she, haughty and
supreme, couldn't give a damn, doesn't notice anyone. But, for Vinicius, what matters is not whether
she sees her admirers or not – the simple fact of her
passing by fills the whole world with grace, and
makes it more beautiful because of love: a literal
translation of his words. Vinicius's lyric, with all its
romantic idealism (Vinicius, who so wanted to be a
Marxist!), is a hymn to beauty as a means of
redeeming the world; not to the pride and self-
sufficiency of a woman who walks around breaking
hearts.

The 'Girl from Ipanema' label, in Portuguese or
English, seems to be everywhere, not always with
the authorisation or knowledge of its owners. It's
the name of a park and a bar in Rio, a boutique in
São Paulo, a swimwear shop in Los Angeles, a
beauty contest in Miami, a Brazilian restaurant
in Milan and even a mare that won a 1,400-metre
race in Bombay. It's the musical backing of an ad
for potato crisps on American TV, and somewhere
in the Caribbean, the name of a cocktail made from
curaçao, pineapple and – poor girl – a miniature

coloured umbrella. Internet prostitution sites, in their hundreds, display photos of 'girls from Ipanema', even if the girls aren't from Ipanema, nor carioca; it's doubtful if they're even Brazilian.

'The Girl from Ipanema' can be found on the Internet in the most unlikely contexts. A doctor from Hong Kong writes about the supposed harmful effects of the sun, and uses the girl as an example, hinting that, with all the time she spends tanning herself, she must have had eighteen or twenty skin cancers by now. Another doctor, American this time, says that he's never been able to listen to the song since a colleague told him he used it to remember the name of the micro-organism that causes syphilis: 'The Girl with Treponema'. Netsurfers in the US, Japan and Germany remember where they were and what they felt when they heard 'The Girl from Ipanema' for the first time – as with the assassination of John F. Kennedy on 22 November 1963. The association may have something to do with it: the original single of Getz and Astrud was launched in New York only a fortnight after Kennedy's death, and there are Americans who listen to it as a theme tune for a kind of 'goodbye to Camelot'; they had their backs turned to what was going on, and ignorance was bliss.

Other surfers love to tell how they came to Rio and seduced the 'girl from Ipanema' – that is, they fell in love with a girl they'd met in Ipanema, took her to their home country and married her. Or married in Rio and stayed here. As the subject is a bit vague – after all, who is the girl from Ipanema? – there's a site given over to discussing just that: 'Who is the girl from Ipanema?' The majority of those discussing this question agree that it really is Helô Pinheiro, the young girl with blue eyes and hair that in those days was black, who, in 1962, Tom Jobim and Vinicius de Moraes saw pass by in front of the bar where they were having a beer, in Ipanema – and, according to the legend, they got their pens out and wrote the music and the lyric there and then.

Tourists are fed on legends, and since the song appeared, the travel agencies, in Brazil and abroad, have used the girl to sell Rio. Among the options offered to visitors, there's a trip to Ipanema beach and to the famous bar, with a promise of seeing 'where Jobim and Moraes wrote the song'. Well, the beach is always worth a visit – cariocas themselves, who've got it all year round, hardly leave the place. And the bar, once a bit rough and called Veloso, but since cleaned and renamed Garota de Ipanema, does really exist, and its owner proudly exhibits the table where Jobim and Vinicius liked to sit. (I've sat at that table with Jobim – me and half the population of Rio, that is, though not on the same day.) But what would the tourists say if they knew that Jobim and Vinicius were serious men who went to the bar to drink, not to work, and that the song was really written long afterwards, miles away, each one in his own home?

As for the girl from Ipanema, of course she exists.

She always did – even before Ipanema was there. She is the true heiress of the girls who, more than a century before, in 1850, walked down the Rua do Ouvidor, when the street was Rio's 'beach'. In this sense, when Vinicius and Jobim focussed their inspiration on a girl from that part of the city, they were paying homage to a carioca tradition that went a long way back, from the nineteenth century, when women had won the right to come and go in a society that, only a short time before, had nearly locked them in their bedrooms.

The fascinating thing is that those pioneers of 1862 did this on territory that was originally 'masculine', as the Rua do Ouvidor was, and managed to draw even with the men. At the beginning of the twentieth century, when the Rua do Ouvidor lost some of its importance and the city grew in the direction of its southern beaches, there was a fascinating change in the area over which they ruled: female toing and froing moved from the street to the sands. There, women found themselves in supremely favourable territory – because, on the beach, free of corsets and petticoats, they could exploit their natural and exclusive arsenal to the full. Once that's understood, the emergence of a 'girl from Ipanema' at some future time was simply inevitable. When this future arrived, and the girl appeared, behold: carioca man saw that she was good (to look at).

But who was this girl, when it came down to it? She wasn't just one, she was many, from the first intrepid creatures who, in the 1940s, began to move from the already busy Copacabana beach to the then distant and almost deserted Arpoador, the beach next to Ipanema. Not all those girls were Brazilian. Some were French, German, Italian, English, Swiss or Danish – these came from the first families to install themselves in Ipanema. They had in common an open-mindedness, an intellectual curiosity and a hunger for living which were almost prohibitive – Vinicius knew them all, and made love to some; Jobim, fourteen years his junior, at least got to know their daughters. For more than twenty years thereafter, for two generations until the middle of the sixties, these women, on the beaches and in the bars of Ipanema, hung out and shared their lives with the typical denizens of the place: fishermen, sportsmen, poets, diplomats, journalists, columnists, musicians, architects, painters, photographers, cartoonists – men of every age and background, but for the most part well-read and informed, eccentric, unconventional. They all benefited from this mixture: the girls, by what they learned from the men, and the men . . . Well, not even Sartre in the Café de Flore had goddesses at his feet to compare with them.

Invisible to the world and to Brazil itself, Ipanema between 1950 and 1965 reproduced on a smaller scale the cultural ferment of Saint-Germain-des-Prés or Greenwich Village. With a significant difference in its favour: it was by the sea, everybody half-naked with the sunshine on their backs and grains of sand getting between the pages of the copies of Françoise Sagan's *Bonjour tristesse*, which the girls took to the beach to read. In fact, the international equivalent at the time would be Saint-Tropez. There was no Bardot or Vadim, but there was the advantage that, in Ipanema, the beach was surrounded by a metropolis, not a fishing village.

The girls from Ipanema in the fifties didn't just want to go out to work, they dreamt of having creative jobs – a large number of them would forge their careers in painting and sculpture, cinema, the theatre, popular music, literature and the press. Long before the Pill and the motel, they already had a sexual life and didn't need to pose as vamps. If anyone thought they were 'easy', they had another think coming – they were very difficult. They made their own minds up. If they liked someone, they went to bed with them, with no fear, guilt or quid pro quo, but the others hadn't the least chance. They might have been a minority in those days, but this was the great difference Vinicius noticed when, just before 1960, he and Jobim began to produce their extraordinary clutch of songs. At that time, the woman who was the subject of the lyrics in Brazilian popular music was *fatale*, nocturnal, unsmiling, treacherous, with a black negligee, her cigarette filter red with her lipstick. Based on what he saw in Ipanema, Vinicius transformed this woman into an adolescent, the lover, the modern girl, golden from the beach, soft but well able to look after herself. Jobim's music went along with this idea, and this explains why the bossa nova was always lighter, more sunny, and, why not, more 'feminine'. The song 'Garota de Ipanema' wasn't this girl's entry into the world. It was just her masterpiece.

This happened decades ago, and from then on, in the eyes of the world, the 'girl from Ipanema' – or the character she represents – has been a kind of paradigm of the carioca woman: pretty, active, articulate, smelling of good soap, with an infallible sense of humour, and mistress of her own existence. Even in Brazil, that's the way she's idealised. But today one can say that, with adaptations, the 'girl from Ipanema' is all over the country. The degree of freedom she won, sweating in her bikini on the beach from sunrise to sunset, has been passed on, buckshee, to millions of Brazilian women. Over time, it has even re-educated the men, and made Brazil an incredibly permissive place.

The permissiveness extends to television, to the family, and to politics. This is a country in which the presidents of the Republic can have lovers or children out of wedlock, in which one of them is photographed from below in a box at Carnival holding hands with a woman with no underwear on, in which an important (female) Minister of State gets involved in an absurd public affair with a married colleague – and the population give these stories their proper treatment: as jokes. In Brazil, presidents don't have an easy time of it – but for other reasons, not because they put their willy where they shouldn't have. If the comic Clinton v. Lewinsky case, which dragged on for years in the

US, had happened here, it would never have led to an attempt at impeachment, and wouldn't have occupied the headlines for more than a few weeks. You could argue that a US president's willy is more important than any Brazilian president's, and you might be right – but only on a world scale. In terms of local politics, two willies have an exactly equivalent weight: which, here in Rio, is no weight at all.

CHAPTER FOUR

Strange things happened in the early months of 2002, when Rio mounted an exhibition, 'The Egypt of the Pharaohs', sent by the Louvre. The show contained eighty-eight pieces, including mummies, sarcophagi, sculptures, jewels and other objects, and, in the starring role, two sphinxes weighing forty tons apiece. It was put on at the Casa França-Brasil, a centre for cultural exchange between the two countries. For the two months it was showing, everything went as it should: 150,000 cariocas came, and there wasn't a single case of an allergy or a sneezing-fit brought on by the age of the pieces. The exhibition coincided with Carnival, and, inevitably, inspired a cheerful, colourful *bloco* called Mighty Isis, founded by the then President of the institution, Dalva Lazaroni. The *bloco* left from the Casa França-Brasil, and went on a lively procession round the local streets. The show was a great success, the French were delighted, in fact everyone was pleased. The problems started in April, when the exhibition ended and the objects were packed to be sent back to Paris.

First, the forklift truck that was supposed to lift the containers broke down. Days later, when that problem was resolved, the batteries in the trucks that were to be used to carry them were found to be flat. When they had been changed, the containers were taken to the plane, but it turned out to have a fault no one could mend, and refused to take off. The curators of the exhibition, serious Egyptologists, laughed and said that the objects 'didn't want to leave Rio'. But when they remembered where and how the show had been mounted, they stopped laughing – it might seem a daft idea, but it could have some foundation.

It begins with the building that houses the Casa França-Brasil. It was the first neo-classical building in Rio, constructed in 1819 by the French architect Grandjean de Montigny used by a pioneering Brazilian stock exchange, and later for customs and excise. Montigny was one of the members of the French Artistic Mission that set up shop in Rio in 1816 at the invitation of Dom João VI. So far, so good. The only thing was that, when he was still in France, Montigny was the architect detailed to restore the sphinxes that Napoleon had brought back from his disastrous Egyptian campaign: the same sphinxes that, almost 200 years later, ended up in the Casa França-Brasil exhibition. Maybe, in that environment, they had 'felt' the loving hands of the man who had repaired the damage done by Napoleon when he removed them from their pedestals in Egypt and took them on the bumpy road to the Louvre. Did they 'miss' Grandjean? Nonsense, you'll say. But who knows? There's no messing with that Egyptian stuff.

As if this wasn't enough, the exhibition had been set up to give the visitor the illusion of entering an Egyptian temple. The curators realised that, at midday, the April sun in Rio, coming in through the skylight of the Casa França-Brasil, projected a ray on to the sculpture of the Sun-King precisely at the same angle as in the temples of ancient Egypt – who knows if the Sun-King hadn't been touched by this gesture? They'd noticed, too, that they'd never seen the mummies looking as robust and full of life as in the Casa França-Brasil. Maybe, too, the Carnival process in honour of Isis had awoken memories of old pagan festivals – after all, Carnival began in Egypt.

Egyptologists believe in 'energies', you know. With so much positive energy in the air, it wasn't impossible that the mummies wanted to stay here, and were 'causing' these accidents. But, inexorably, the fault in the plane was mended and they had to go back, kicking and screaming.

Cariocas also feel comfortable with the embrace of the past. In Rio, you turn a street corner, and a different century appears before your eyes, in the form of an aqueduct, a façade, a building, or, less often, a group of buildings. In a country that still thinks of itself as a spotty adolescent, Rio is proud of being an 'old' city, its long career reflected in its architectural variety. This diversity goes from baroque churches, forts and convents of the colonial period (1565–1808) to innumerable examples of neo-classicism (nineteenth century), eclecticism (the first thirty years of the twentieth century) and modernism (from the forties onwards), culminating in the latest postmodernist stupidities – all these styles spread with no planning throughout the city, living together in relative harmony, and sometimes, cheek by jowl.

Not to mention secondary styles: not much is left of art nouveau, but, for anyone fond of art deco (I love it myself), Rio is a huge repository of the style. There are buildings in which, from the lift-foyer to the rooms themselves, you'd think you were in the black and white sets that Van Nest Polglase made for the RKO Fred Astaire and Ginger Rogers movies – only they are for real, authentic, with solid walls and tiny subtle details in the finishing touches. There's nothing strange about this. The building boom in whole neighbourhoods like Glória, Flamengo, Urca and Copacabana in the thirties coincided with the worldwide peak of the fashion for art deco. That was why Rio acquired so many buildings, houses, and even churches with those typical nautical lines, undulating and aerodynamic, which sit so well with the curves of the mountains. We need look no further than the statue of Christ the Redeemer, created by the engineer Heitor da Silva Costa, which is a phenomenal art deco monument.

The presence of the past might have been more all-embracing, were it not for the mania of Brazilians – an eternally 'young' nation, frivolous and playful – for despising everything that's more than fifteen years old (or fifteen minutes, for that matter). Rio has suffered from this, because, in the three centuries it was the country's capital, the city wasn't allowed to be mistress of her own fate: during the Monarchy and the Republic, all the mayors were appointed by the federal government – it was only from 1985 onwards that cariocas had the right to elect their own mayors! With each change of government or regime (and heaven knows, these things change often enough round here), Rio, as the country's shop window, had to be subjected to a thoroughgoing reform so that the new rulers could show their own style off. Almost always, this meant demolishing the past.

What is left of colonial Rio is a miracle when you think of all that did exist and was destroyed or left to rot. In 1920, the Morro do Castelo (the hill where the city, still based on medieval models, really began in the sixteenth century) was flattened by dynamite and water-hoses, along with practically everything that was on top of it: the city's first houses (dozens of them), a curtain wall, two forts, a hospital, a convent, a church, and Estácio de Sá's grave (luckily they removed his remains and a few religious ornaments, and took them elsewhere). The argument was that the hill impeded the circulation of air in the Centre of the city. In fact, what they wanted was space to build – so much so that, years later, when the esplanade that appeared where the hill had once been was given a bunch of modernist buildings higher than the original hill, no one suffocated. As for the earth removed when the hill was taken down, it was used to choke off the arm of the sea between Villegagnon island – yes, the very same – and the mainland, so allowing the building of Santos-Dumont airport.

In 1944, the opening of the Avenida Presidente Vargas, eighty yards wide and two and a half miles long, destroyed 500 old houses, including three 300-year-old churches and, what was even more tragic for the city, put paid to the area where the carioca blacks had made history: the Praça Onze. The idea was for the new Avenida to become a business centre. But the city, which is a bit unco-operative when it comes to taking orders, went in the opposite direction, because what's there now is a collection of empty spaces where, at night, only angels and fools dare to tread. The construction of the Avenida also separated the city from the old port area of Saúde and Gamboa, where, in the seventeenth and eighteenth centuries, bits of Brazil were taken to Europe by ship, and Africa came here in return. Another harmless hill that was knocked down around 1970, Santo Antônio, opened up a space for buildings that would win any competition in bad taste. The worst of them, the new Metro-politan Cathedral, is a vast bucket turned upside down, reminding one of a nuclear power station –

and the more deserving of being blown up for having made the Lapa Arches (in the eighteenth century, the biggest building in the Americas) look absurdly tiny.

In the name of hygiene, progress and modernisation, and all the wonders they are supposed to bring, megalomaniacs equipped with two deadly weapons – a pencil and a blank sheet of paper – have persuaded Rio's rulers to level a good part of the city's heritage. Not everything was lost. But that's only because, having listened to some apparently brilliant proposal, someone sometimes asked themselves if it might not in fact be idiotic after all. If all the lunatic projects submitted to the mayors of Rio had been carried out, several of the city's symbols would have been consigned to the dustbin and we wouldn't have the city as we know it.

In 1886, a French visitor, the Viscount de Courcy, proposed nothing less than knocking down the Sugar Loaf to solve the problem of lack of ventilation in the centre – caused, according to him, by the narrow entrance to Guanabara bay. If the Sugar Loaf evaporated, the city would be able to breathe freely and the outbreaks of yellow fever which plagued it would end. It would be costly, he recognised, but the high cost could be financed by the sale of the stone, not in fragments for souvenirs, but in blocks, for buildings the size of the pyramids. The Viscount was not an expert in public health, city planning or geology. He was just a dilettante, an amateur of *belles lettres*, and all the more dangerous for that – even more for being French, which meant that he must have had an enthusiastic Brazilian audience drinking in his every word. To his disappointment, no one took him seriously, and the Sugar Loaf was permitted to go on existing. As for yellow fever, along with smallpox and typhus, it would be defeated some years later by the carioca sanitation expert, Oswaldo Cruz, with a much more effective instrument – vaccination.

In 1929, another Frenchman, Le Corbusier, on his way through Rio, worked on a new urban project for the city. One of his ideas was the construction of a viaduct on stilts – a gigantic centipede which would wind its way above the streets, climbing up or tunnelling through the hills, in a huge curve parallel to the coastline, extending from the Centre of the city to Leblon. But don't faint with horror just yet. It was to be a housing-viaduct, for all along the motorway there were to be fifteen floors of apartments with capacity for 90,000 inhabitants, as well as ramps, garages, lifts for cars and a hangar for seaplanes. At various points, the housing-viaduct would throw out legs or arms which would invade the neighbourhoods more distant from the sea, like Lapa, Laranjeiras and Lagoa. It would have made the Great Wall of China look like the balcony on a pagoda.

The fact that such a monster ever got to be dreamt up, turned into a sketch and seriously dis-cussed round a table by men with waxed mous-taches, makes one shudder. I can just imagine the

Avenida Beira-Mar, with its symmetrical English gardens, then still young and fresh, my beloved Flamengo beach, the voluptuous contours of the Morro da Viúva, Botafogo bay, the Avenida Atlântica, also fresh and new in those days (and already with its Portuguese paving in wave-formation, inspired by the pavements in Lisbon), the young, almost pre-pubescent Ipanema and Leblon; all these milestones innocently glorying in their rightness and beauty – while, in an office with its windows shut, men were discussing their destruction, perhaps without even intending it. Maybe they didn't yet know that a slow and painful death awaits anything with a viaduct built over it.

Or perhaps they did know? In his justification for this project, Le Corbusier wrote that, when he saw Rio from the plane window, and saw that it was a city that 'seems to dispense with any human collaboration, with its beauty universally proclaimed, [he] was possessed by a violent, perhaps even a mad desire to try out a human adventure here – the desire to play a game for two, on the one side *human affirmation*, on the other the *presence of nature*'.

This is the fate of certain cities. The more blessed they are by a sensational setting, the more they kindle in architects the desire to compete with that same scenario. Why was Le Corbusier never gripped by a 'a violent, perhaps even a mad desire' to play a 'game for two' with, let's say, Caracas, Manchester or Detroit? (No offence meant.) And it would be fascinating to see him try the same thing on his own city, Paris – the mere notion of a concrete worm winding above the Place Vendôme or the Bois de Boulogne would be enough for him to be put in a straitjacket. In Rio, they listened attentively to his explanation and served him coffee and a glass of water. Luckily, in 1930, Brazil was the setting for a revolution that altered the country's political system, and as the new government had other priorities, the project was filed.

In 1936, Lucio Costa, one of Le Corbusier's many Brazilian disciples, proposed the Rodrigo de Freitas lagoon as the site for the University City they wanted to build in Rio. No, it wouldn't be necessary to fill the lagoon in. The university would float over the water, which would act as a mirror. The buildings would stand on stilts – stilts again – with gardens on the roofs, 'for strolling between classes', and huge awnings to protect them from the sun; all this linked by bridges and viaducts – always viaducts. This project was described by Lucio Costa in a letter to Le Corbusier and submitted to the then Minister of Education, Gustavo Capanema. But, for some reason, happily, it was not carried out. The University City was built in another place, far away, and the lagoon was saved – as those cariocas know who run, cycle and walk hand in hand along its banks, sail on its waters and look across it to the other side without a Fritz Lang set getting in the way.

And the Maracanã stadium? It should have been

quite different from the one that was finally built for the 1950 World Cup and, in spite of a few amputations, survives to this day. The idea of building it came from the 1938 Cup in France, when FIFA laid it down that one of the next few competitions would be in Brazil. Then Rio made up its mind that it would construct a big stadium. The first studies were made and two things were decided: one, that it would have room for more than 100,000 people; and two, it would be in the Maracanã neighbourhood, on a piece of land where, in the past, there had been a racetrack. In 1941, the carioca Prefecture launched a competition for the project and several architects entered. All the plans were rejected. One of them, by the young Oscar Niemeyer, proposed that, to avoid the spectators having to go up ramps, the stands should be at street level – and the pitch, forty feet down.

That's right, forty feet. You can imagine what a revolution in football that would have created. In this pan buried in the ground, without a breath of wind and heated by 150,000 mouths, the famous *Fla-Flus* [derby games between Flamengo and Fluminense] would be played in a temperature of 50° C; quite apart from the fact that the Maracanã area is prone to dramatic floods – any heavy rain sets them off. If it had been built to these specifications, the stadium would have become, periodically, the biggest swimming pool on earth. The water would have cascaded down over the seats, spread over the standing area, filled the ditch separating the spectators from the ground, covered the grass and filled the underground dressing rooms, drowning the players and the fleeing masseurs. Faced with this possibility, Brazilian football would have had to adjust – perhaps it would have been played with flippers instead of boots – and it would have been very different from the game that in the future would give us Garrincha, Pelé, Tostão, Zico, and Romário. We might not have become five-times champions of the world. As the writer and journalist Sérgio Augusto said, at the outside we might have become five-times champions in water polo.

But good sense didn't always win out. In 1976, during the military dictatorship, a historic building right in the middle of the city was demolished at the personal caprice of the general on duty at the time. This was the Monroe Palace, built in 1904 in the United States to serve as the Brazilian pavilion in a world exhibition in St Louis, Missouri. Though it was constructed on American soil, with local materials and labour, it was a truly Brazilian building, in the eclectic style, designed and built by the military engineer Francisco de Souza Aguiar – and it was planned that, when the exhibition was over, the metal structure, the façade, the cupolas and the decoration would all be shipped to Rio, in pieces, and reconstructed in the most prestigious part of the city, the Avenida Central. This happened, in 1906.

In the first decades of its existence, the Monroe

was Brazil's reception room, and hosted several international congresses. In 1925, it became the seat of the Federal Senate, and for the next thirty-five years, everything of any importance in the political life of the Republic happened there. It was also beautiful, and formed, with the Opera, the central Law Courts, the National Library (also designed by Souza Aguiar) and the National Gallery of Art, a group of buildings that became one of the symbols of the city. In 1926, basing his plans on this group and closing the quadrilateral of Floriano Square, the entrepreneur Francisco Serrador built Cinelândia, Rio's celebrated open-air catwalk, with its eleven cinemas, three theatres, four hotels, big department store, nightclubs, ice cream parlours, cafés and tobacconists, full of people day and night – a very carioca reply to Damon Runyon's Times Square. It was the Monroe, with its politicians who came to Rio to get civilised, that presided over this quadrilateral. Its image decorated the back of Brazilian banknotes, and went all the way round the world on stamps and postcards, as well as acting as the back projection for the conspiracies between Cary Grant and Ingrid Bergman in *Notorious* (1946), Alfred Hitchcock's film whose action takes place in Rio.

In 1960, with the change of capital, the Senate was moved to Brasília. But the Monroe kept an extra-official status – many senators preferred to carry on their business in Rio, which was still Brazil's real political capital. In the seventies, the worst years of the military dictatorship, the General-Presidents, in their blind urge to neutralise the city's rebellious nature, deactivated the Monroe and abandoned it. In 1974, when the carioca metro was being built, it was found that, according to the engineers' plans for the area, the Monroe's foundations would get in the way. Either the metro would have to go round it in a curve, at 'prohibitive' cost, or the building would have to be destroyed. Guess which was the government's preferred solution.

When it became known that the Monroe was in danger, people mobilised to save it. Engineers, historians, art critics, town planners, landscape architects, politicians and ordinary people, united in their love for the city, passionately protested in defence of the building. Several organisations offered to occupy it and even restore it, but bureaucratic problems got in the way. In the campaign in favour of demolition were the newspaper *O Globo*, two or three pitiless modernist architects, and, inexplicably, some organisations set up to 'protect' our historical and cultural heritage. Their arguments were that the Monroe had no historical or architectural value, and that a garden with a fountain in it would be better in its place – although it was already one of the areas of the city with most gardens, next to the Passeio Público, the Praça Paris and Flamengo park.

The fight for the Monroe dragged on for more than a year, during which time the firm undertaking the construction of the metro stopped asking for its destruction and made the tunnel go round it – even taking care to protect the building's foundations with stakes, so that the work wouldn't undermine it. But even this didn't save the Monroe. Its demolition seemed to have become the obsession of half a dozen people. Finally, the decision was left in the hands of one man: the then Dictator-President, General Ernesto Geisel. Geisel voted for demolition.

In January 1976, the stained-glass windows of the main chamber (one of them of fifteen square yards, representing the proclamation of the Republic) began to be taken down. For the next three months, before the mystified eyes of the population, the three bronze cupolas were dismounted, along with the Carrara marble lions at its front entrance, the jacaranda doors, the blocks of the parquet floor, made of *peroba* wood, the Riga pinewood panels, the wrought-iron staircase, the statues, the furniture, the railings. With each piece that was taken away, there were more appeals for the demolition to be stopped. 'There's still time to save the Monroe,' 200 engineers and architects proclaimed, in a manifesto. But it was useless. When the walls, made of mortar boiled with whale oil, began to shatter from the blows of sledgehammers and rock crushers, everyone realised it was the end. And, even if the destruction had been stopped, the parts had already been dispersed – as the federal government took no interest in buying them, they were sold to individuals from several Brazilian states, and even from Japan. They went to decorate restaurants, hotels, motels, offices and plantation houses in the remotest parts of the country.

Even now, decades after its destruction, its parts are still in circulation. In 2000, one of the Monroe's doors – nine feet by five, and seven centimetres thick, full of inlay work and bas-reliefs, still with its original German locks and latch – reappeared in a deposit of demolition material in Salvador, Bahia, 1,030 miles from its original habitation. It was bought at auction by a friend of mine, the carioca painter Leonel Brayner, for a studio he was building in Bahia. Hardly believing what he had in his hands, Leonel didn't just install it. He made the architect redo the whole plan and made the studio to fit the door. Because of this, the height of the house itself, of which the studio was an annexe, had to be adjusted. It must be the only building in Bahia made for a door. But for Leonel, who loves Rio, and like me is one of the Monroe's orphans, it was the least he could do. In his dreams, the Palace is still standing, in the same place, and occupied by honest, worthy politicians dedicated to the good of the country.

The destruction of the Monroe was one of the great crimes committed against Rio – perhaps the military regime wanted to destroy the city's political culture. Or, even pettier, the general who happened to be on the throne had an ancient quarrel with a fellow officer, son of the military engineer who had built the Palace. Nothing was ever proved – it was the dictatorship, after all – but it's generally believed that, to satisfy his monumental spite, Geisel could find nothing better to do than authorise the destruction of a monument.

Because of this, Rio has to stay the way it is: on its toes all the time. When rulers, technicians and speculators get together to talk about it, the earth begins to tremble. The seagulls scream, the sea throws sand on to the streets, a waiter spills beer on to his tray, and I feel shivers up my spine.

Tom Jobim used to say that the best way of going round New York was on a hospital trolley. In Rio, the ideal vehicles are your feet – on the asphalt or the sand – and literature. The two usually go together: few cities make such good characters, have given the names of muses to the streets, or produce so many authors who write with their feet; it's just a pity that they write in invisible ink – in Portuguese, I mean.

In 1862, shortly after Baudelaire invented the Parisian *flâneur*, the gentle carioca writer Joaquim Manuel de Macedo published his book *A Walk Around the City of Rio de Janeiro*. It was the same Baudelairean idler, the same aimless wandering, and Rio also encouraged it. It is true that Macedo did it with pencil and notebook in hand, which does break the *flâneur*'s rules, or so it seems to me. (But are there any writers who are pure *flâneurs*, wandering round the streets determined *not* to write?) In 1878, he returned to the streets with *Memoirs of the Rua do Ouvidor*, limiting the territory of his *flânerie* to one only – but one which was 300 years old and had become Brazil's main thoroughfare. Macedo's Rio was as mild and benign as he was, almost unrecognisably placid. Perhaps because Macedo only went to places where he wouldn't muddy his gaiters; fights between the police and *capoeiras*, public punishments for rebellious slaves, Frenchwomen dancing the cancan in the low-life vaudeville Alcazar theatre – none of these works of the devil ever dared cross his path. Don't jump to conclusions, however: Macedo's Rio did exist, and maybe it was possible to live in it without coming into contact with the rest.

The Rio of the writer and journalist João do Rio was quite different. The streets didn't attract him for what they showed, but for what they concealed. In 1908, he published a book whose title might be the definitive formula for literary *flânerie*: *The Enchanting Soul of the Streets*. Only the book didn't quite correspond to the suggestion in the title: the soul was not to be found in the flowery, perfumed streets of Laranjeiras, but in the labyrinth of dark, twisting, dangerous alleyways around the port. João do Rio infiltrated the shadiest dens in the city, and revealed a human flora in an advanced state of decomposition: murderers, opium-smokers, drug-dealers, *macumba*-adepts, ruffians, professional beggars, jailbirds, tattoo-artists, prostitutes, street-children – the fascinating cast of people that every great city, whether it wants to or not, ends up producing to make up for the excess of upright citizens, respecters of the law. It must have been difficult for João do Rio to go to these places without being noticed: he was fat, mulatto, with a shaven chin when the rule was a beard and moustache, as well as a homosexual and a dandy, always to be seen with a colourful suit and a monocle. For him, wandering round the underworld was small beer: as a reporter, he was always going into these catacombs; as a human being, he was a discreet night-time *habitué* of the Praça Tiradentes, then a gay area. He was also very popular – when the American dancer Isadora Duncan came to Rio in 1915, he was her guide and the two were applauded together in the streets as they went by. Few writers like João do Rio have lived and written so intensely about what he called the 'neurosis' of the modern city. When he died of a heart attack in a taxi, in 1921 at the age of forty, his funeral brought the city to a standstill.

In 1938, another chronicler of the city, Luiz Edmundo, turned his memory round and, walking it slowly through the streets, reconstituted the city of the year 1900 in *Rio de Janeiro in My Time*, a Brazilian classic in the *flâneur* genre. When he published the book, Luiz Edmundo was sixty, had a long career as a journalist behind him, and had a sparkling memory – of course, he was helped by a large amount of research into the past, but his book wouldn't have been so exciting if he hadn't known the places and people he described. Luiz himself, as a character, is conspicuously absent from his story, although he could easily have played his own part: twenty-two years old in 1900, he was a poet, a bohemian, at ease with the literary and political bigwigs of the time, beloved in the Café Colombo and the Lamas restaurant, and a competent exponent of the 'cake-walk', the fashionable dance at the time. If the reader lets Luiz Edmundo take him back to the past, he wears out his shoe-leather: he walks along the streets, sits down in the squares, goes up on to the hills, gets the tram, tries out dishes in restaurants, goes into all kinds of environments (nearly suffocating in some of them), is introduced to a large number of people (the really important ones and the mere windbags), hears all kinds of accents, and, such is Edmundo's descriptive power, breathes in the scents and the stinks of the city. There's no nostalgia in Luiz Edmundo: when he takes the reader by the hand, he also takes him through what is ugly, dirty and outdated; the reader has to take care of himself.

From the *flâneur*'s point of view, in any city in the world, no time can have been as congenial to healthy idling as those placid, lyrical years between 1890 and 1914, later called the belle époque. Everything was in its favour. The cities were smaller – they might be metropolises, but the megalopolis had not yet arrived. The streets were reasonably well lit and paved. Almost all the buildings were on a human scale (in New York they only got to twenty floors with the Flatiron, on 23rd Street, Broadway and Fifth Avenue, in 1902). Cars were rare or non-existent – there were no car-parks, only carriage-ports. The main means of transport, the tram, even when it was electric, rolled along in harmony with your heartbeat. And any decent citizen could mentally undress a woman as she passed by, without risking arrest for sexual harassment.

Of these cities, none seemed as placid and lyrical as Rio. You could walk in comfort through the streets in the centre. There was music in the air, from the pianos near the windows, from bands on their bandstands, from barrel organs and even from knife-grinders. On the pavements outside the cafés, writers wielded *bons mots* as girls went by swinging their bustles, caught in the subtle web of a metaphor. You went to football in a straw boater, stiff collar, a pearl in your cravat and wielding a stick – sticks were necessary for masculine aplomb, and were useful too for resolving little tiffs involving questions of honour. A president of the Republic could go by tram, alone, from home to his office and back, mixing with ordinary people, without anyone bothering him. All this, beside a bay which, seen from above by the birds, put never-never land into a cocked hat.

Aside from this, what other city could pride itself that its first motor accident had been caused by . . . a poet? Not just any poet, but the most famous one in the country: Olavo Bilac, author of a line – 'What, you'll say to me, hear the stars?' ['*Ora, direis, ouvir estrelas?*'], which caused cardiac arrest in all the sexes. Bilac's poetry was almost scientifically rigorous, but, in 1902, when he tried to drive the first and then only automobile in town, he forgot to ask the difference between the brake and the accelerator. He simply borrowed the car from his friend, the journalist José do Patrocínio, turned the crankshaft, ran to the driving seat and hit the first tree in his way. There were no casualties, apart from the car and the tree.

But, if belle époque Rio seems so placid and lyrical to us these days, it's basically because we can only see its romantic side. Most of the moving pictures filmed since 1898 have been lost, and we have to be content with stills; however marvellous and abundant they are, they're also static, fixed, as if the city were posing for a picture postcard, and always trying to show its best profile. To get behind it, we have to look at history; at times there was nothing placid or lyrical about it.

In September 1893, the city was struck by the cannon shots exchanged between the ships manoeuvring in the bay, under the command of the rebel admiral Custódio de Melo, and the land forces loyal to the President, Marshal Floriano Peixoto. This was the Naval Revolt – right here in never-never land. The admirals wanted to depose Floriano, and usurp the Presidency themselves. By day, the rebel battleships, cruisers, torpedo boats, gunboats, frigates and corvettes took aim at the forts manned by the government. At night, the pro-Floriano searchlights swept the bay, and the forts took aim at the rebel ships, sinking some. In the crossfire stood the city of Rio, with its church towers, its convents on top of the hills, and a few somewhat higher buildings. During one of the attacks, the customs (the future Casa França-Brasil) was hit; on another occasion, a fuel deposit blew up on the Ilha do Governador; and on yet another, a stray missile – a cannonball – knocked the tower of the church of the Lapa dos Mercadores in the Rua do Ouvidor down, setting fire to the building next door. If you wanted to go idling round the streets in those days, it was a good idea to keep your eye on the sea and the sky.

When either side attacked the other, the people ran to the Central do Brasil railway stations, to get the trains that left Rio every ten minutes. In the middle of the bay, right in the line of fire, the French, British, Italian, Portuguese and American merchant ships tried to keep away from the cannon-fire. None were hit, but some were rooting for Custódio, others for Floriano, and if they'd taken part in the ruckus, the conflict would have taken on an international dimension. The revolt went on into the new year, and in February 1894, seriously affected Carnival. In April, without the reinforcements it had hoped for, the navy surrendered. Its leaders went into exile and many people were arrested – among them Bilac himself, a fanatic opponent of Floriano. The skirmishes had lasted for seven months, leaving about 100 dead and 300 wounded, among them civilians, women and children. Peace returned to the city, but it was a warning: what would have happened if things had *really* hotted up? Just for the record: the President who went on the tram back and forth to work – in the midst of the crisis – was Marshal Floriano.

Ten years later, in 1904, another rebellion spoilt the idyllic postcard image. This was the Vaccine Revolt. At the beginning of the century, Rio's major problem was not the favelas, but the horizontal *cortiços* in the area around the centre – horrifically poor collective lodgings, with a population at the mercy of ailments like yellow fever, smallpox and typhus. It was more or less like Paris in 1857, before Haussmann, the East End of London in 1888 when Jack the Ripper flourished, or New York's Lower East Side in 1900. Almost every city had pestilential areas, and governments, still by and large ignoring the social problems, concentrated on so-called 'hygienist' solutions – you had to confiscate and flatten crumbling buildings, disinfect the area and build all over again. In 1904, after innumerable projects that never left the drawing board, Rio started a serious programme of reconstruction and sanitation.

The pickaxes and hammers rang out in the city for two years, destroying thousands of miserable shacks and expelling people who had no other choice but to go up on to the hills to live. Rats were hunted and killed by the ton in the poor streets, while brigades of mosquito-destroyers ransacked the low-class neighbourhoods, fumigating every drainpipe and potted fern. Construction took over the city. When the scaffolding finally came down in 1906, Rio was reborn, airy, modern and 'European', with wide illuminated avenues, seaside promenades, a quay for transatlantic ships to dock, and beautiful buildings with lifts and doormen. At last it was a city worthy of its natural setting. A French poet, Jeanne Catulle-Mendès, called it: '*La ville merveilleuse*'. The man responsible for the reforms was the Prefect Pereira Passos, an engineer who had seen the reconstruction of Paris by Eugène Haussmann. In charge of sanitation was his Health Secretary, doctor Oswaldo Cruz, thirty-two, an ex-pupil of Louis Pasteur.

While it was just a matter of hunting for rats or killing mosquitoes, Oswaldo Cruz had the people's support. But when he imposed compulsory vaccination against smallpox, he faced the most violent incomprehension of any doctor of his day: a revolt in which the enraged poor seemed, incredibly, to be on the side of the disease. Years before, similar protests had occurred in England and the United States, and for the same reasons. But in Rio, in November 1904, they caused seven days and nights of violent chaos in the streets, with the destruction of lampposts, the burning of trams, attacks on the vehicles of the sanitation services, the looting of warehouses, knife and pistol fights between the population and the police, which left many dead and wounded. Even Oswaldo Cruz was threatened in public. It was one of the biggest popular revolts in the history of the city and the only one that for a long time defied understanding.

Now we know that, in the perspective of that time, it would have been strange if there had been *no* protest. As they saw things, humble men and women were being forced by the hated police to bare their arm or leg so that strangers (the sanitary agents) could give them a prick which left a scar and through which was injected an unknown liquid – many thought that the vaccines were being used to kill the poor, and that what was being injected was the illness itself. Of course that wasn't so, but in an uneducated environment, President Rodrigues Alves's opponents, among them military men and trade unionists, used this belief as a political weapon: they encouraged demonstrations, incited the revolt in the papers, and gave it an absurd dimension.

Oswaldo Cruz succeeded in imposing his campaign, but he died, thirteen years later, still embittered by the incomprehension. His posthumous victory, however, was complete. People became aware of his greatness and turned him into a national hero. The Manguinhos Institute (now the Oswaldo Cruz Foundation Institute) created by him has educated successive generations of public health experts, and become a world-renowned research centre on the subject. Years later, as soon as the bathing costumes started shrinking on Rio's beaches, there wasn't a single carioca girl who didn't show a delicate vaccine mark on her thigh or buttock.

In November 1910, when Rio was again pristine and Guanabara bay was never-never land as never before, the waters got choppy again with another revolt: carioca sailors rebelled against the punishment meted out to them, took their officers prisoner and occupied the ships anchored in the bay. The revolt, headed by the able seaman João Cândido Felisberto, started on board the battleship *Minas Gerais*, and the spark that set it off was the punishment of 250 lashes handed out to one of the sailors – thus the name of the revolt, the Whip Revolt [*Revolta da Chibata* – the *chibata* was a whip with nails in it]. During the taking of the *Minas Gerais*, her commander, the naval captain Batista das Neves, faced the mutineers with his sword and died for the sake of hierarchy. There were deaths, too, on the other ships.

The sailors pointed the cannons at the Catete Palace, the seat of government, and made their demands: the abolition of corporal punishment, a wage rise, improvement in the food on board, reduction of their time of service, and an amnesty for the rebels. (It was a more ambitious programme than that of the men on the battleship *Potemkin*, who only revolted against the quality of the meat used by the cook.) That list would have been enough of an affront for the officers, but there was something about the revolt that disgusted them even more: João Cândido and ninety per cent of his

2,000 insurgents were black, and in the Brazilian navy as in most others, blacks were not allowed above deck – much less could they give orders to their 'racial superiors'. The officers tried to surround the rebel ships, mining the entrance to the bay so that they couldn't get out. But the sailors saw through the manoeuvre and, to prove this was no game, took aim at the Morro do Castelo, causing two deaths. As in the revolt of 1893, Rio was in danger of finding itself in the middle of a shoot-out, with its people, once again, taking the brunt.

Under pressure from the Senate, President Hermes da Fonseca (the future husband of Nair de Teffé) conceded the amnesty and put his spectacles on to analyse the demands. The sailors accepted the truce, handed themselves over to the officers, and insisted on giving them back the ships with their decks just washed. But, straight away, using a revolt on the Ilha das Cobras as a pretext, the government suspended the amnesty, declared a state of siege, attacked the mutineers, killed hundreds of them and arrested many, including João Cândido. Eighteen of the leaders of the revolt were thrown into a tiny ship's hold and sent to Amazonia. Sixteen died on the journey, asphyxiated in this cubicle, and two were saved by breathing through a tiny hole in the hull – one of them was João Cândido. He served his sentence and lived until 1969, when he was eighty-nine, still in time to see the *chibata* abolished, and to be acclaimed as the 'black admiral'.

It really *was* a belle époque, and the city *was* a *flâneur*'s dream. It was just that there were a few little local difficulties.

A hundred years have passed, and the Rio of Joaquim Manuel de Macedo, Luiz Edmundo or João do Rio is long gone. The city has grown in every direction, and what these writers thought of as Rio (the area between Glória and the Campo de Santana, where the majority of cariocas lived, worked and amused themselves in the nineteenth century) soon became just the Centre. Little by little, it ceased to be residential, but in every other sense, it was still where Rio really happened. So much so that cariocas went on calling it 'The City'. Not even the old chroniclers imagined that its golden age was only just beginning.

For decades to follow, more than half of the twentieth century, this square mile and a bit was a distillation of the whole country. It was where both houses of Congress, the ministries, the head-quarters of industry, of the banks, of financial institutions and political parties, of commerce, the newspapers, radio stations, recording studios, publishers, bookshops, fashion houses, hotels, res-taurants, theatres, cinemas, dance halls (high and low class), brothels, bars, cafés, whatever you wanted were – from the richest, most gleaming establishments to the darkest and most secret. Its characters were men and women of the world, whose lives revolved around these palaces of power and pleasure, under the gaze of a critical, good-humoured entity, with a relaxed moral sense – the people of Rio. And nearby, there was the Lapa neighbourhood, which was a world apart.

The sheer weight of its institutions seemed to make the Centre impregnable. Power was there to be seen, in its buildings with their massive columns, high walls and monumental façades. Going into one of these to look for a document was like going into an Assyrian palace in the reign of Ashurbanipal. The Avenida Rio Branco (formerly Central) was the country's backbone – a coffee drunk on one of its corners could affect the product's international price. But when it came down to it, it was found that the area's defences were fragile. With the move of the capital to Brasília in 1960 and the political, administrative and financial strangulation of Rio after the military coup in 1964, it was the first place where the evidence of asphyxia could be seen.

Imagine a host who puts a family up with all the luxury it deserves – and the guest decides to leave, 300 years later, taking everything that was put in place to receive him, leaving the host with nothing but the walls, and that if he is lucky. The host was Rio and the guest, the Brazilian government in its various incarnations. Little by little, the federal bodies based in Rio were deactivated (or, if they were left here, with a few exceptions, they were on a diet of bread and water). Reluctantly, banks moved to other places. Industries decayed, even the shipbuilding industry, and the docks were transformed into a graveyard of useless machinery, condemning an enormous area to death. Huge numbers of businesses shut. Of the no fewer than twenty-one daily newspapers circulating in Rio in 1960 (and they all had their editorial offices in the Centre), fourteen died in the next twenty years. Of the fifteen weekly magazines, none have survived. Even the diplomatic corps, which resisted the move for ten years (and rightly: Rio was regarded as one of the most desirable postings) ended up having to go to Brasília. The whole city felt the blow, but the Centre was the worst hit. The stage-set was still there, but it was decaying fast, and its new occupants followed the pattern – instead of marchionesses and magnates, there came vagabonds, the unemployed, the poor.

In an ideal Brazil, the centre of Rio should have been turned into an open-air museum as soon as the leaders of the Republic began to leave for Brasília. Unfortunately nobody thought about it, and even if they had, it would have been impracticable: how can you conserve a museum with two million people milling around in it every day? Not to mention the venerable public collections, archives and repositories that tell the country's history, which left the city – and are still leaving to this day; God knows where to. The only reason the Centre isn't completely disfigured is that, without ever abandoning it as the city's hub, Rio moved towards the beaches, and everything in the area lost value: the businesses, the buildings, the clientele. It wasn't worth knocking things down to rebuild. One way and another, the offices went on operating (those that survived the innumerable crises of the Brazilian economy), as did some of the businesses around them, though they were now in competition with street-traders. But the excitement of the area's nightlife collapsed – its streets and squares, which in the first half of the twentieth century were bursting with people into the wee hours, became a no-man's-land as soon as the last executive or secretary took their car or bus to the Zona Sul or the Zona Norte.

It does depend what you mean by no-man's-land. In his story 'The Art of Walking in the Streets of Rio de Janeiro', Rubem Fonseca made his character wander at dawn through the ghost-city the Centre had become. The settings still recalled those of Joaquim Manuel de Macedo and Luiz Edmundo, but what he found in the streets were successors of João do Rio's characters: idlers, toothless whores, pimps, drug-dealers, graffiti-artists, transvestites, street-salesmen, preachers of the gospel, people coming for the striptease shows or the porno movies – the kind of people you wouldn't exactly think of inviting to tea with your maiden aunt. It was fiction, but grimly close to reality. Cities, unlike novels and plays, don't choose their own cast-list.

From 1970 on, everyone who could leave the Centre did so. And those who went there in the daytime only went out of professional duty. It was cruel and unjust because, in spite of its visible impoverishment, the Centre still offered many of its old pleasures: fish in the Albamar restaurant, draught beer at the Bar Luiz, imported goods at Lidador's, the popular dances at the Estudantina, the Leonardo da Vinci bookshop, the National Library, the Real Gabinete Português de Leitura, [Royal Portuguese Reading Room], the second-hand bookshops, museums, churches, tea shops and whisky bars. It is true that, suddenly, certain contrasts began to stand out: the remains of traditional, gracious, almost feminine kind of shops – selling hats and parasols, for instance, or small opticians, confectioners and sweet shops – looked even more fragile in the midst of the harsh new surroundings.

I never got used to it. While many of my acquaintances in the Zona Sul prided themselves that they hadn't set foot in the Centre for years, I went on wandering round there in the eighties, hoping that, when I walked along one of those sordid streets, I might come out in a past made shiny and new again. It never happened – but it was moving to see how, however much it was assailed, in every way, that past wouldn't go away.

Behind the façades of the institutions the government had left behind when it moved to Brasília, in empty storeys of abandoned buildings, you could see decorative brick floors, painted panels, carved furniture, grooved columns, crystal chandeliers, wrought-iron or carved wood staircases, ceilings with garlanded friezes, coloured glass skylights,

everything that hadn't been taken away or robbed –
walking through those interiors, even if the sun was
coming through the windows, required a musical
backing on the theremin by Miklos Rozsa. They
were *pentimenti* of the great days when visitors
walked through there – some of them, indeed, lived
there – people like Anatole France, Enrico Caruso,
Paul Claudel, Albert Einstein, Frank Lloyd Wright,
Marie Curie, Thomas Mann, Rudyard Kipling,
Stefan Zweig, Orson Welles, Darius Milhaud, Al-
dous Huxley, André Malraux, Albert Camus, John
Dos Passos, Graham Greene, Jean-Paul Sartre,
scientists, musicians, writers – the name-dropping
could fill the rest of the book. (The novelist Sherwood Anderson, on his way to Rio, died of peri-
tonitis on the high seas when he nibbled a titbit and
swallowed a toothpick.) Not counting the political
chiefs, industrial tycoons, bankers, diplomats and
tourists who disembarked daily, from ships, planes
and even dirigibles. Rio's sumptuous past – the
quantity of money that the Centre of the city
generated and the taste with which that money
was used – was imprinted on those interiors. It
wasn't transferred to the cities the money migrated
to.

But this is not the story of a phantasmagoria, and I
have much pleasure in informing you that, just as it
is no longer the world of Macedo or Luiz Edmundo,
the old Centre of Rio is no longer that of Rubem
Fonseca's story. Just when you least expected it, life,

youth and future returned. There were lots of people who, without making too much fuss about it, and instead of just walking round the city as I did, hands in pockets, kicking bottle-tops and cursing the dereliction, wanted to 'do something'. And they knew what to do.

In 1979 a group linked to the Prefecture realised that, with its cultural legacy in ruins, Rio was in danger. The risk was all the greater in that, unlike Ouro Preto, Paraty, Olinda and other *bijoux* that have kept a colonial architectural unity, Rio was not considered a 'historic city' by the Brazilian cultural heritage authorities – because it is very big, uneven and 'disfigured'. That is, by prioritising architecture (and even then, their usual favourites: colonial and modernist), the bureaucrats in these departments were voting against history. It didn't matter to them that every century of Brazilian history, especially the nineteenth, was engraved on the Rio streets and that even the scars disfiguring it told that story. So Rio concluded that if it wanted to save itself, it could count on no one but itself.

The idea came from the architect Augusto Ivan de Freitas Pinheiro, then Secretary for Planning of the Rio Prefecture: the creation of a 'cultural corridor', that is, listing dozens of monuments, forming conservation areas around them, and recuperating, inside and out, 1,600 old buildings in the legendary streets and squares of the city. More daring yet: all this without a cent of government money, relying only on the goodwill of the owners of the buildings and businesses – in the early years, they weren't even promised tax exemption on the side.

Strange, but true. Augusto Ivan and a handful of brave men and women decided to ask hundreds of people, comfortably off or not, to put their hands in their pockets to restore their properties, or undo the hideous 'improvements' that had altered them over a period of a hundred years. In exchange, the Prefecture would look after the streets, which was no more than its duty. But, in the not-so-long term, they promised, everyone would benefit. This was no longing for a dead past: the object wasn't to reinvent the 'old Rio' of the nostalgia-freaks, but to re-equip it for the present and offer it to the young, who didn't even know it existed. It was a deliciously romantic idea, a dream – ideal, perhaps, for some city in Germany, Switzerland or Holland. But in Rio??? You could hear the laughter on the Amazon or the Uruguayan border.

It looked impossible, and it took five years just to get beyond the planning stage – but it was done. A team of architects, historians, writers (one of them Rubem Fonseca), artists, designers, popular music critics – all of them bohemians and familiar with the city's seamier side – took to the streets. They all knocked on doors, in different neighbourhoods in the Centre, trying to convince shopkeepers and landlords to restore their houses and façades according to the original plans and colours. To this end, they showed old photos and engravings, talked about the building's past, and often brought surprises with them. The owner of a building on the Rua do Lavradio, for instance, was delighted to know that, around 1830, Dom Pedro I used the rooms as a love nest. Just as in this case, only then did the owners realise their building's pedigree, hidden under horrendous plastic signs or behind a wall that shouldn't have been there at all. When this hand-to-hand fighting began, in 1984, no one knew when or if it would end. They just hoped the Centre wouldn't die first.

One owner might resist the changes, but he might well subscribe to them if his neighbour bought the idea. Little by little, the results began to come, and they got enthusiastic. By around 1990, whole blocks had been reborn, with their façades newly restored to the beauty they had had when they were spanking new in 1890. This without excessive purism: the interiors could be 'modern', so long as they didn't interfere with the spirit of the construction. Businessmen started taking a fresh interest in the area, and in places that had lately been the haunt of rogues and scoundrels – like the Ruas da Carioca, do Lavradio, do Teatro, the Arco do Telles and the Praça Tiradentes – there appeared antique shops, restaurants, dance academies, art galleries, design shops, photographers' studios, book publishers and bars with live music, as well as cultural centres, both large and small. Not that I've anything against rogues and scoundrels, but why should the city belong to them alone?

Rio responded to these initiatives, and nowadays,

a lot of the Centre is alive with young people in the early hours, every day of the week. Places which had long been abandoned have taken on a second life. Nightlife has even come back to the Lapa; inside the big houses and on the pavements outside, they today have music, draught beer and salt-cod balls, in the same streets – Joaquim Silva, Conde de Laje, Visconde de Maranguape, Lavradio, Mem de Sá – which, in the past, gave the neighbourhood its name as the quintessence of bohemia, and a very carioca mixture of Montmartre and Pigalle.

The resurrection of the Lapa has something symbolic about it. For the long years when it was officially dead, it was as if Rio kept an unburied body in the back room – the body of a wild, whoremongering genius of an uncle. During this period, while the body lay around stinking, the Lapa was the subject of books, sambas and theses which sang of its history and lamented its passing. No other neighbourhood of the city was the object of so much nostalgia, and rightly so, because not many had as much history.

From 1900 to the Second World War, night-time in the Lapa gathered all the able-bodied men in Rio: socialites, writers, journalists, painters, musicians, politicians, judges, lawyers, spivs. The professions and the bank accounts might vary, but there, no one was better than anyone else, except by the standards imposed by the Lapa itself – from the smart set in their dinner jackets, just come down from their parties in Santa Teresa, to the ruffians with their black shirts, white ties and winkle-pickers. Lapa contained sin and redemption side by side; its fifteen streets, alleys and steps up the hillside were divided by the Arches (almost sacred for cariocas), blessed by a church (the Lapa do Desterro, built in 1751), and crowned by a convent (the Carmelites). While the nuns dedicated themselves to prayer, pleasure took its course into the early morning. There were the deluxe cabarets, with walls of mirrors and an orchestra on the mezzanine; the *cafés-chantants*, one of them presided over by a female baritone; there were restaurants open round the clock, with girls serving food prepared with a Portuguese, German, Polish, or Hungarian accent; in the adjacent Glória, there were casinos like the High-Life and the Beira-Mar, which featured shows starring Josephine Baker, all the better to fleece the innocent. The sheet anchor of all this, giving it its spirit, were the brothels – a huge number of them.

Some of them were no expense spared, with art nouveau washbasins, lilac lampshades, red velvet curtains and, on the gramophone, Lucienne Boyer singing '*Parlez-moi d'amour*'; there was one belonging to Raymonde, a Frenchwoman, which even provided its clients with the latest number of the *Nouvelle Revue Française*. Others were on a more modest scale, with a whiff of cheap perfume. The prostitutes were of various nationalities, but they all wanted to pass as French (for this reason, they read novels by Colette between clients). Many were

Polish Jews and had landed up there through a white slave traffic system set up in Europe. Some of the Lapa women married millionaires and plantation owners from other states and disappeared from Rio, obliterating their 'past'. Sometimes a prostitute would kill herself, drinking champagne with ant poison and leaving behind that most unexpected of messages: a love letter.

A multitude of honest professionals depended on the Lapa: taxi-drivers, bouncers, doormen, waiters, cleaners (in the brothels, almost always homosexuals), cooks, cabaret artists, musicians, croupiers. The people there were quick on the uptake – a shoeshiner, while he was polishing up two worthies having a casual conversation, might have got hold of a valuable bit of information, just by keeping his ears open. All the establishments had live music, though, in spite of the legend, samba wasn't the Lapa's forte – mostly they played waltzes, opera selections, French songs, tangos, foxtrots and gypsy tunes. Because of the large number of intellectuals, sex and poetry perfumed the atmosphere: poems by Villon and Rimbaud were declaimed by the clients in the cabarets, sometimes between doses of so-called 'alcoloids' – morphine and cocaine, sold under the counter in some of the neighbourhood chemists, or by discreet dealers. But only a minority took their chances with these things – most people stuck to beer, vermouth, whisky, and, on special occasions, Veuve Cliquot. The Lapa was reputed to be violent, though its *habitués* could never understand this: it was a rare event for ruffians, like the famous Meia-Noite [Midnight] and Camisa Preta [Black Shirt], to get into a knife-fight – generally, anyone could come and go in the Lapa with their patent-leather hair intact.

Even so, in 1940, the Chief of the Federal Police, Colonel Etchegoyen, decided to clean the area up. With all the delicacy of Attila the Hun, he shut the brothels down, drove the prostitutes out, persecuted the madams and the homosexuals. The girls, who had till then been kept in fixed areas, spread throughout the city, and the Lapa was left to the 'polite families' who lived there too (mine, for example) and took no part in the upheaval. Without the brothels, the clients disappeared, the cabarets went into decline and closed, and all the area's commerce was harmed. The Lapa became fossilised as a poor, melancholy neighbourhood which went to bed early, except for a few stray ladies who returned and set themselves up in modest rendezvous. The bohemian world, attracted by the casinos and later by the nightclubs, moved to Copacabana. The Lapa was moribund for nearly half a century, during which some blocks were knocked down and replaced by large empty spaces, typical of an arrogant town planning just as empty of real content. Even a heroic initiative, like the opening of the Cecília Meirelles Concert Hall in 1965, looked out of place in its desolate surroundings. The garage of the *Correio da Manhã*, from which, for almost seventy years, cars left carrying reporters bent on overthrowing ministers, became a parking place for popcorn sellers' carts. There were humiliations like that all over the area. How could anyone imagine that one day the Lapa could be reborn in such a spectacular fashion?

But, beginning with shows in the *Circo Voador* [Flying Circus] and by the parties in the *Fundição Progresso* [Progress Foundry] in the eighties, that was what happened. The body in the back room was finally buried. The big houses were opened, and shaking off its decades-long attack of the blues, the Lapa got light, sound, and a whole new population. The settings today remind one of yesteryear, with just a slight coat of varnish on the decay; the same can be said of the nights, which enliven the place so wonderfully.

But there are differences between the old and the new Lapa. In the former, the protagonists were overwhelmingly men – the women were at their service. In the new Lapa, truth to tell, there isn't even prostitution. Young men and women of every class mix in twenty or so houses with live music, sing, dance, get bladdered, share the bill and have a good time together. On a weekend night, it's quite usual for 5,000 people, native and tourist, to be jammed into the bars and the heaving streets, where samba, *choro*, *forró*, funk, and other rhythms seem to come at you from all over the place. All that's left of the old magic is the smell of piss on the walls. The official uniform for the lads is a pair of bermudas. None of them know who Villon was (though they'd like him if they did), and their drink, apart from draught beer, is a *xiboquinha* – a concoction of *cachaça*, honey, cloves, cinnamon, peanuts and other lethal weapons, sold on the streets at almost no *reals* a shot.

As the Lapa has got too small for the multitude, the tumult has overflowed into the nearby Praça Tiradentes and its surroundings, shaking up theatres and dance halls dating from when the future carioca soprano Bidu Sayão (1902–1999), who was brought up there, had a kiss curl and didn't even dream of being of a star at the New York Metropolitan. From the Praça Tiradentes, one gang of carioca night owls has spilt over into the Rua da Carioca, where two cinemas, the Iris and the Ideal, which almost go back as far as Edison and Lumière, now house as many as 1,500 young people for parties that go on past eight in the morning – I don't know how they don't collapse from the beat coming out of the loudspeakers. Six or seven blocks away, in the direction of the corner of the Ruas Visconde de Inhaúma and Miguel Couto, is the Sardine Triangle, a complex of six bars with acres of tables on the pavements. There, as the name implies, no one could die of lack of fried sardines – or 'sea chickens' as they call them, because of the way they're served, open like chicken breasts. The clientele of this area must be Belgian – well anyhow, they look as if they could come from either Brussels or the Congo. Going westwards now, towards the Candelária church, there are cultural centres surrounded by another flood of open-air tables which, pushing along the romantically cobbled streets, empties into the Arco do Telles in the Praça Quinze de Novembro. And, to complete the bohemian rectangle, we come back to Cinelândia, which is also going through the beginnings of a revival, perhaps because it's the younger brother of the place where it all began: the Lapa.

When it's put that way, you might think that the historical Centre of Rio is being cleaned out so that cariocas can drink beer, eat junk, listen to samba, and chat around grimy bar tables, while they appreciate the female gluteal muscles that press by them on their way to the toilets. What if it is? The bars are committee rooms for discussing and keeping an eye on the city – and they have the advantage of seeming to be in permanent session. Also, one thing there's no lack of in Rio are seminars to discuss Bakhtin, Barthes and Foucault. But none of these conclaves are far from dives where the subject might be, let's say, football, and sometimes, it's the same Foucault experts who debate the fates of the city's clubs: Flamengo, Vasco da Gama, Fluminense and Botafogo. It's a more transcendent affair than you might imagine, because it involves the feelings of tens of millions – the carioca clubs have fans all over the country, and the supporters of Flamengo and Vasco are greater in number than the populations of many European countries.

Rio has respectable scholars, professionals and bohemians. However, often these three qualifications are present in a single person. The economist Carlos Lessa, an eminent Brazilian intellectual, is proud to be a founder of the Carnival *bloco Minerva Assanhada* [Randy Minerva]. The ex-federal-deputy Luiz Alfredo Salomão, of the Workers' Party, used to finish his work in Brasília and take the plane to Rio in time to play the drums in a samba group. The beautiful standard-bearer Selminha 'Sorriso' [Smile], a star of the *Beija-Flor* samba school, is a driver for the carioca fire services. Being serious about their work doesn't stop them living their lives too.

When you think about it, why this prejudice against bars? In Rio, bar – *botequim* – is a concept embracing luxury restaurants, like the Antiquarius, the Cipriani or the Saint-Honoré, where whiskies under the age of twenty-five are not allowed in, as much as corner dives, with their own pet flies, a little red light over a picture of St George, and people sitting on beer-barrels on the pavement or just standing, with their elbows on the bar. Everything is a bar. Snobs may turn up their noses, but the idea, as well as being inspiring in its own right, has illustrious antecedents. Christianity was born round a table in Jerusalem, with thirteen men drinking wine and exchanging proverbs. In the Middle Ages, the best European families defined themselves as such by bashing mugs on a round table and wiping their mouths with the backs of their hands. Without the literary bohemia of the cafés of the Palais Royal, maybe there'd have been no French Revolution – that was where they were when they left, a little tipsy, to flatten the Bastille. Even Lenin said goodbye to the bar opposite his house, the Cabaret Voltaire in Zurich, where he played chess with the Dadaists, and got that famous train to the Finland Station. In Rio too, lots of events had their origins at a bar table, though none were important enough to speed up the planet. The nearest example one can find is the story (false, as we already know) that Jobim and Vinicius wrote 'The Girl from Ipanema' at a table at Veloso's bar.

The bar is an institution so central to life in Rio that the guides to the city's restaurants, published annually, include many of them. This doesn't stop them having their own guides (also annual, and supported by the Prefecture); books are beginning to appear, too, exclusively dedicated to some of the most illustrious, like the Jobi, the Bip-Bip or the Bar Lagoa. Nowadays, several of the bars are listed buildings, either because their architecture is worth preserving, or because they contain a part of the city's cultural or historic heritage – or both things at the same time, like the Bar Luiz, which goes back to 1887, and was the place where Rio exchanged wine, a Portuguese custom, for draught beer (so much more carioca).

Before it was too late, Rio spent the last twenty years listing everything it could, including things you'd think no one could tamper with, like the Sugar Loaf, Christ the Redeemer, islands, monuments, groups of important buildings, porticoes, balustrades and even trees. But nothing is that obvious in Rio, and, if there's a chink in the armour, greedy builders go right in and, in the middle of the night, knock down a 300-year old building. Till a short time ago, the federal agencies only thought things that looked baroque or rococo were worthy of preservation. Influenced by its historians, Rio has widened its horizons, and nowadays, among other landmarks to be rightly protected are the trams and tramlines of Santa Teresa, the hangar for dirigibles at the Santa Cruz Air Base (the Graf Zeppelin and the Hindenburg could often be seen in the sky over the city), the tenements and steps of Saúde, the pavements in Vila Isabel (in which the Portuguese cobblestones form the notes of classic sambas, the indomitable Copacabana Palace, the oils by the kitsch painter Nilton Bravo in the bars, the head-quarters of the *Bola Preta* [Black Ball] *bloco* in Cinelândia, and even Pepê's stall in the Barra da Tijuca.

But the parameters should be widened still further. If it was down to me, intangible things, things difficult to lay your hands on but which sum the city up, would be listed: carioca speech (a synthesis of every Brazilian dialect, with echoes of the long familiarity with the Portuguese spoken in Portugal and also with French), good humour (which nothing seems to destroy, not even the city's periodic crises), and incredible resourcefulness (centuries of struggle against all kinds of problems have taught cariocas how to get by to live). If this seems a little unconventional for the heritage authorities, I'd be contented with listing more concrete things, like the sunset seen from the Arpoador, the Old Guard of the samba schools (made up of men and women over seventy, as elegant as you can imagine, who should have their hands kissed every day, not just at Carnival), and the city's sun-worshipping, responsible for its mental and physical health (in Copacabana's morning sun, it's really hard to imagine those skeletal figures, more dead than alive, with studded black leather clothes, hair standing on end and a nappy-pin in their cheek).

I'd also list everything that cariocas call, delightfully and proudly, 'low cuisine'. Many cities are quite rightly proud of having all the world's haute cuisine in their restaurants. Rio doesn't go that far, though the Brazilian equivalent of the Michelin Guides, the *Guia Quatro Rodas*, regularly votes three or four of its restaurants among the seven best in the country. What makes a cuisine irresistible is its good, cheap, everyday food, like the croque-monsieurs served in any Parisian snack bar; the little dishes of mussels and squid in Madrid's tapas bars; and, in New York, the hot dogs from the steaming carts on Sixth Avenue, with the executives taking care not to drip mustard on their Ermenegildo Zegna ties – even the hamburgers at P.J. Clark's are cordon bleu cuisine.

Rio's forte are the typical dishes served in bars, almost always enough to feed two people for twenty-four hours, and which cast a suspicious light on Third World hunger statistics. When I get the menu at one of these establishments, I feel like getting up on a chair and declaiming it as if it was something by Machado de Assis or Eça de Queiroz: oxtail and watercress, goat with rice and broccoli, gnocchi with beef olives, pork loin with butter-beans and *farofa*, dried beef with manioc porridge, pork shank with cheese and pineapple, minced beef with rice, *farofa*, banana and fried egg. The names of the dishes themselves are an ode to cholesterol, but who wants to live for ever? Not to mention the inexorable *churrasco à Oswaldo Aranha*, invented in the twenties in the Cosmopolita in the Lapa, which is still the best place to eat it: a formidable thick steak, covered with garlic, accompanied by rice, *farofa* and chips. A hint from the real con-noisseurs of these culinary torpedoes: if you *really* want to eat well, look for a bar with a taxi rank in front – taxi-drivers *really* know how to eat. Another hint: don't be guided by silly prejudice. The best liver in the city, for example, can be found in a bar in the Praça da Cruz Vermelha.

The apex of carioca low cuisine, however, can be found in the savoury snacks served in bars: little balls of manioc or salt cod, prawn and cheese pasties, shredded dried meat with onions, *lingüiça* [a sausage similar to chorizo] by the yard, bean gravy with pork scratchings, and innumerable other sins. These snacks are the bars' real pride and joy. They are refined gluttony, if you'll allow me the contradiction. And a carioca is yet to be born who is indifferent to Globo biscuits, which have been sold for fifty years on the beaches and the streets; they have already saved many lives, particularly of people caught in traffic jams between lunch and dinner.

But the masterpiece of carioca cuisine, something like a symphony for drums, is, naturally, *feijoada*, which has been practised here since the mid eighteenth century by the slaves, and later was adopted by their masters. Everyone's love of this dish makes any unfavourable comments irrelevant; one example of the latter was attributed to Jean-Paul Sartre, in 1960, in the house of a Rio journalist. When they lifted the lid off the pan where a tremendous *feijoada* was simmering, Sartre is supposed to have examined the contents – a festival of black beans enriched with bacon, ribs, the ears, tongue and tail of the pig, dried beef, *lingüiça* and *paio* [another kind of sausage] – and rudely exclaimed: '*Mais . . . c'est de la merde!*' The host, who hadn't expected such a reaction from the author of *La Nausée*, was taken aback. To his surprise, however, Sartre ate it and liked it. And, it is said on the best authority, he had second helpings and ordered his other half, Simone de Beauvoir, to copy out the recipe. It's not mentioned whether, at the door, there stood the accompaniment that Sergio Pôrto regarded as indispensable to a good *feijoada*: an ambulance on call.

The French call orgasm *la petite mort*. *Feijoada*,

by the quasi-orgasmic ecstasy it brings on, is another candidate for that expression.

There's a dialogue in *Casablanca* in which Conrad Veidt, in the role of the ominous German Major Strasser, threatens Humphrey Bogart with a Nazi invasion of New York. Bogart is unperturbed: 'Well, there are certain sections of New York, Major, that I wouldn't advise you to try to invade.' That was 1941. But already then, what might have seemed a privilege exclusive to New York could be applied to the majority of modern cities: they all have areas that are impenetrable, for the exclusive use of antisocial elements who pay no taxes, spend their spare time oiling machine guns, and give a discreet snarl before they say anything. What's not fair is that these same elements sometimes come into the city and mix with honest citizens, but don't react well to being visited in their own lairs, especially by the police.

For centuries, Rio has taken its beauty, its history and its quality of life for granted. Whole buildings had to disappear, neighbourhoods die on their feet, the *morros* be cleared of vegetation by chaotic, piecemeal occupation and organised crime rule the roost in the streets for cariocas to become aware that everything is linked together – and that, if the city stops belonging to them it will be given over to others, who will use it for purposes incompatible with life itself. And it's not in the carioca lifestyle to sit at home watching life on television. The Lapa is an example: it was dark, gloomy and threatening. Now it's a part of the city, and you can walk round it with your eyes closed (or almost, because a little tension is part of its charm). Following its example, too, other areas have been reborn. A few more years, for instance, and the Monroe wouldn't have been destroyed – because I and many others would have chained ourselves to the lions.

A general awareness has grown up that, whatever other serious measures are taken, Rio has a great future behind it: the proper valuation of its heritage. It's one of the few big cities in the world where there are still things to be saved. Thanks to the process set in motion by Pinheiro's Cultural Corridor, the city now has about 10,000 protected buildings – the majority of them in the area where the old journalists like João do Rio wandered. But it's still not enough, for, around them, there are another 20,000 unprotected, and some even in danger of collapse.

If every city is, metaphorically, an urban jungle, Rio has done something much more difficult than recuperate neighbourhoods or buildings. It has reconstructed a whole jungle – a real one – inside its urban limits: the Floresta da Tijuca. It did this at a time, the second half of the nineteenth century, when the word ecology wasn't in the dictionaries and the life of a tree was worth as much as that of a worm, maybe less.

Anyone who walks through the Floresta today will find it hard to believe that, in 1861, it was a huge coffee plantation, whose owners were English and French, with a few burnt or charred areas to relieve the monotony. The original forest, with its wonderful wild vegetation, had almost completely given way to coffee and the wood and charcoal industries. Can you imagine jacarandas being cut down to make fences or going to the oven to feed locomotives or flat irons? That was what happened. Not everyone was insensitive to the devastation – one man, the Viscount of Bom Retiro, fought for years for the salvation of Tijuca. Nature itself didn't enjoy the way it was being treated, and whenever it could, got its own back by drying up the springs that sprang up on its sides and provided Rio with water. In December 1861, after a series of droughts and several frustrated attempts to stop the destruction, the Emperor Dom Pedro II confiscated plantations, created the forest and appointed one man, Manuel Archer, to oversee the replanting.

For the following eleven years, Archer lived in what, one day, would be the forest. Helped by six slaves (Eleutério, Constantino, Manuel, Mateus, Leopoldo, and one woman, Maria), he cleared and prepared every square metre of land and planted a record number (100,000) of cuttings. At the start, they had to come from Paineiras (near the top of the Corcovado), from the Passeio Público or Guaratiba, brought on mule-back or by the slaves – it took years for Archer to have his own nurseries on Tijuca itself. Adult trees were planted only to give shade to protect the more delicate saplings. When they took root and grew, the trees were reused, and new cuttings planted in their place. For a long time, Archer had to fight against the hostility of the earth itself, punished as it had been for the previous hundred years. Even so, the death-rate of his trees was minimal. Archer also created the process of planting small cuttings in bamboo baskets, waiting for them to grow and only then planting them properly in the earth. And nature played its part, exuberantly expanding and using whatever he had planted. We could call the resurrection of the Floresta da Tijuca a miniature version of a day of creation – a day that took eleven years.

One detail: Archer wasn't a botanist, he was an engineer. During the time he worked in the forest, he had ranged against him a drought that almost ruined everything, as well as ministers who tried to sabotage him, and cuts in his budget caused by the Paraguayan War. But in 1874, when he resigned to go and replant the forest around Petrópolis, his Floresta da Tijuca was a reality.

If Archer had been a conductor, his idea of an orchestra would have been to mix the violins with the trumpets, the harps with the tubas, put the cymbals in with the flutes, and tell them all to play in unison. That was what he did with the *ipês*, jacarandas, palms, ironwoods, bamboos, *muricis*, *sapucaias* and wild orange trees, among dozens of species he planted, cheek by jowl. But what music his forest played! (Apart from guaranteeing Rio a water supply much better than what had been there previously.) His successor, the Baron de Escragnolle, continued his work and dedicated himself to beautifying the forest, controlling its waterfalls, constructing bridges, grottos and belvederes, and putting French sculptures along its alleyways. And then, when everything seemed to be moving towards a happy ending, the old Brazil came back into the frame: with the death of Escragnolle in 1888 and the coming of the Republic a year later, the forest was abandoned – because it had been recuperated 'by the Monarchy'. For the next forty-four years, the vegetation was left to grow in complete chaos, the buildings were reduced to ruins, and some began to chop the trees down again. Kicked from ministry to ministry, no one knows why the forest didn't die.

In 1943, another great carioca, the businessman Raymundo Ottoni de Castro Maya, decided to rescue it. Castro Maya cleared the excess plant-life, restored all the equipment (including Archer and Escragnolle's original houses, which became the Floresta and Esquilo restaurants), created new viewing terraces, opened paths and provided its museums and chapels with works of art. Four years later, in 1947, he transformed the forest into a public park, now listed by the city, and a shock for any foreigner who visits it. The Americans are the most surprised, when they find that it is the biggest urban forest in the world, made by men, and that *nine* Central Parks would fit into its

32.5 square kilometres – Central Park being only 3.6 square kilometres. They are even more shocked when they are told that the Floresta da Tijuca is *not* included in UNESCO's world heritage sites.

Spread between Rio's beaches and streets, the forest stands guardian over mysteries we will never penetrate. Seen from here, below, it is a silent, solemn counterpoint to the city's own mysteries – which are not at all solemn or silent.

CHAPTER FIVE

There's not a chance of a carioca going out without taking a shower first. On a realistic estimate, we can guarantee that an adult carioca has 1,000 showers a year – an achievement that, on other continents, many would take a lifetime to equal. It might seem too much, but it's not. It works out at 2.73 a day, a lower average than the ancient Tupinambás reached on weekdays. But it is a respectable amount, and one of the reasons for their untiring dedication is that, between the decision to get into the shower and the actual shower itself, cariocas don't have many clothes to take off. A fair proportion of the population spends its days in shorts or bermudas, even at work, and there are innumerable jobs which allow this extra comfort with no loss of professional face: bus conductor, ice-cream seller, peanut vendor, fisherman, soap-star, gangster, lifesaver, beach salesman, tourist guide, kids who juggle at the street lights to earn coppers, pop singers at parties, fashion stylists, photographers, architects, painters, foreign newspaper correspondents, and even some successful

businessmen who don't have to go to the city
Centre, visit bankers or be beholden to anyone.
Writers, too – even me. Or the novelist João
Ubaldo Ribeiro, who only takes off the bermudas
he wears when he walks round the streets of
Leblon to put on the ceremonial uniform of the
Brazilian Academy of Letters.

Even when Rio is infested with tourists, as at new
year or Carnival, it's easy to find a carioca in the
multitude. He's the one with his legs on show. The
tourists are that way too, but they either wear white
shirts or ones covered with prints of palm-trees,
khaki bermudas, black shoes and white socks that
go halfway up their shins. A carioca never sports
formal shoes with bermudas, much less does he
stretch his socks that way. Usually, in fact, he
doesn't wear socks at all. The same applies to the
women – in the whole of the Western world,
carioca women must be the lowest consumers of
nylon stockings. In Rio, they see no reason to use
them, even at gala evening receptions – it's almost
never cold and their legs already have the colour the
stockings try to imitate. To tell the truth, carioca
women aren't in the least crazy about make-up –
with so much sunshine, who needs Helena Rubin-
stein?

People from outside must be shocked by cariocas'
absolute informality; they don't think twice about
going into an ordinary restaurant in the same
clothes in which they've just come off the beach:
bathing costume, no shirt, in sandals or barefoot,

and with the vestiges of the Atlantic Ocean still on their bodies. It must be astonishing too that, when a couple enter, the waiter quite naturally comes up to the man, gives him the menu and asks what they'll have to drink. The same applies to women in bikinis. Both walk around the restaurant, get up to say hello to well-dressed friends, eat, pay and leave without anyone realising they're almost naked. Cariocas' familiarity with their own bodies must have no parallel in any other metropolitan city. The choreographer Rossella Terranova, who is of Italian origin but lives in Rio, realised this recently when she gave a course on bodily awareness in Milan. When she asked some of her students to take their shoes off, she noticed that for some of them it was embarrassing. 'It was as if they hadn't seen their own feet for months!' she said to me. In Rio, on the other hand, Rossella has given classes for people a short step away from nakedness, and *honi soit qui mal y pense.*

Of course it wasn't always like that, and even cariocas had a struggle to free themselves from the dead weight of clothes that, in denial of the temperature, were imposed by European tradition. In the first half of the nineteenth century, Rio was like a court in a tropical operetta. If he had to go to the Imperial Palace to talk to anything in authority, an ordinary citizen had to put on a three-cornered hat, a fitted topcoat, lace cuffs, breeches tied just below the knee, silk stockings and buckled shoes. Some of them didn't even get inside the building – feeling they were going to faint in the heat, they flung themselves into Mestre Valentim's fountain, and, on contact with the water, their clothes went *fzzzzz*. The city looked like something out of the *Memoirs of a Militia Sergeant* [a comic novel by Manuel Antônio de Almeida, published in 1855], full of grenadiers with uniforms like toy soldiers – or a belated copy of the ancient (1678) novel by Madame de La Fayette, *The Princess of Cleves*. When they went to the theatre, the women balanced two-storey wigs on their heads, and the men couldn't do without powder in their hair. Aristocracy couldn't forgo its airs and graces, even in a tropical steam bath.

But little by little, they had to start getting in touch with their surroundings. In 1831, the installation hairdos were put out of fashion by the salon of the coiffeur Desmarais, on the Rua do Ouvidor. In 1840, straight trousers replaced breeches, and topcoats gave way to jackets. And the young Emperor Pedro II, as soon as he could, exchanged his royal regalia, lined with ermine, for a double-breasted coat: much more civilian and modern.

In the ensuing decades, cariocas started leaving their clothes by the wayside, but they had so many of them that, when the Republic came, on the eve of the twentieth century, they were still as wrapped up as their European cousins. Their clothes were not only heavy, they were dark, as befitted men who thought of themselves as grave and responsible. In 1902, Dr Graça Couto, a medical doctor, shocked all decent families by going out in the street in a white linen suit, with shoes the same colour. If the author of this outrage to decency had been a journalist or a poet, his insolence would have had no repercussion. But Dr Graça Couto was an influential scientist, director of the Society for Hygiene; his colleagues followed him, and were followed in their turn by ministers of state, judges and barristers. It was the signal for cariocas to tidy up their wardrobes once and for all. Carnival, the beach and sport did the rest. Even so, it didn't happen all at once: until 1920, football referees still blew their whistles dressed in jackets; until 1940, no one went to the Centre in shirt sleeves; and until the sixties, you weren't allowed into cinemas in bermudas. But these were tardy, sporadic examples of conservatism: in 1926, in Rio as in New York and Paris, girls dressed in a *melindrosa* (a very short skirt, with a low waistline) on the Avenida Rio Branco. They went without stockings, too, with bare legs, because the beach and the new bathing costumes had already laid down the cult of tanned skin.

The beach was the great watershed. When someone writes the history of beach culture in Rio, its pre-history (leaving aside the Indians) will have to begin in 1808, with the royal family. All its members were adepts of sea bathing, if only to treat their skin complaints. Dom João VI, who lived in São Cristóvão, went to Caju beach – even built a little pier there, making Caju into Brazil's first bathing place. He got into a kind of bath with a hole in the bottom and, still clothed, let the waves break against it. Dom João's unruly wife, Carlota Joaquina, preferred Botafogo beach, on the corner of what is now the Rua Marquês de Abrantes, where she lived. They say she went into the sea naked – not that that would have made much difference to any possible passer-by, since she was famously ugly. Some years on, their son Dom Pedro I and his wife, Dona Leopoldina, went to Flamengo beach, which, much later, was also the favourite of their granddaughter, Princess Isabel. I can imagine Isabel coming out of her home (the future Guanabara Palace), getting into the caleche with her ladies-in-waiting, and driving down between the palm-trees of the Rua Paissandu to the then modest beach at the end of the street.

What a good thing it was that, from early on, the Portuguese were aware that beaches ought to be public, and not divided into little private compartments, as they are in many European countries. When Brazil became independent it began to create its own legislation, but that custom continued, so that ordinary people had access to the beaches in the bay. The problem was that they were no great shakes: narrow, full of stones and with an insignificant little strip of sand. The beaches on the ocean, from Copacabana on, were wonderful, but they were almost secret: they were a long way away, and isolated from the city by mountains.

In 1823, Maria Graham decided she wanted to see the great beach that extended behind the Sugar Loaf. Living as she did in Catete, she got on her horse and took the route of present-day Rua Senador Vergueiro. She went along Botafogo bay, and instead of continuing along Saudade beach (later turned into the Avenida Pasteur), she went round the Morro do Pasmado, till she reached the Estrada Real [Royal Road], which took her to the steep Morro de São João. She took hours to get up it, but finally got to the top. It must have been worth it, because from up there she could contemplate the immense sandy area spanning 5.2 square kilometres, with the curve of the beach, edged by *pitanga* and *jambo* trees, and then more mountains – a festival of white, green and blue set against a light that would have challenged Delacroix himself. This was Copacabana in its virgin splendour, only broken by the little church at its extreme southern end, built in 1776 in honour of Our Lady of Copacabana. Graham was the first writer to allude to Copacabana in a written text, and she didn't forget to mention the armadillos and opossums that lived there, feeding in that landscape.

If today, the sight of the concrete jungle of the Avenida Atlântica still takes your breath away, you can imagine what that wild coastline did for Maria Graham. From her natural belvedere, she could see over the Morro dos Cabritos and the Morro de Cantagalo, and make out behind them the Corcovado, Dois Irmãos, the Pedra da Gávea, and everything that later would be blocked out by the palisade of high-rises. Other visitors followed (German, French, English), and their narratives also describe a Copacabana almost before human beings got there. In 1886 the actress Sarah Bernhardt, then on tour in a Rio theatre, also ventured out there, but she was more daring: she went down to the water, got her feet wet, and – who knows – had a picnic with chicken and *farofa* brought from the Carceler restaurant on the Rua do Ouvidor – for dessert, she'd have had *cambucás* [a sweet yellow fruit like a plum] plucked from a seaside tree.

I know, it seems incredible that cariocas deprived themselves of Copacabana for almost 400 years. For that very reason, there are people who argue that Rio was already perfect before the white men decided to build a city here, in such unsuitable, uneven terrain. Finally, in 1892, the tunnels, trams and the first summer residences opened Copacabana up for common mortals. Innocence was gone. Nature defended itself as well as it could, obstructing the pioneers, but there was no way it could resist human persistence and ingenuity.

In 1902, an English barber in Copacabana, Wallace Green, invented the beach towel without intending to. After shaving a client, he decided to take a break on the beach and, not wanting to dirty his uniform, spread the towel on the beach to sit down – so resolving a serious problem of logistics and starting the fashion. In 1906, the Prefect Pereira Passos built Copacabana's great beachside road: the Avenida Atlântica – and as often as storms destroyed it, even chucking octopuses into the houses, successive prefects rebuilt it. In 1919, the little church, the area's first landmark, was lamentably destroyed to build Copacabana fort. But then history took its revenge. In July 1922, during yet another Brazilian political crisis, eighteen young officers (and one civilian) came out of the same fort and marched along the Avenida Atlântica, to face the machine guns of hundreds of pro-government soldiers. Several did actually die, on the corner of the street that would later be named after one of them (Siqueira Campos – who didn't die there), and their blood baptised the Portuguese stones arranged to form waves that were then being laid on the pavements. This same pavement, after this rather melodramatic baptism, would soon be a byword the world over for excitement and pleasure.

On that same day, five blocks away from the epicentre of the battle, Brazilian and European workers were putting the penultimate touches to the construction of a six-storey hotel in the neo-classical style, planned by the French architect Joseph Gire: the Copacabana Palace. For many, it was just a white elephant in the middle of nowhere. But when the 'Copa' was opened, in 1923 – a hundred years after Maria Graham's excursion – Copacabana inevitably mushroomed around it.

*　　*　　*

'The hotel and its bright tan prayer rug of a beach were one.' That's F. Scott Fitzgerald in *Tender is the Night*, referring to the Carlton Hotel, in Cannes, in the twenties. The words could equally apply to the Copacabana Palace at the same time. Even more so, in fact, for the Copa was born with no rivals for the rug, and had the sea all to itself. It was as if a ship had been beached and left there, silently dominating the landscape.

Its owners, the Guinles, were a Brazilian family of French origin. Their fortune in 1900 was the equivalent, in today's money, of about two billion dollars. The family patriarch, Eduardo Guinle, had made it building docks, hydroelectric schemes, roads, setting up banks and insurance companies, and going into partnership with the British in steel, telephone systems, locomotives, lifts, and typewriters. But Eduardo died in 1912, and his seven children decided to spend his millions in the best way possible: they invested them in glamour. Some of them built luxury hotels, private palaces, parks and gardens in Rio and its outskirts. Some spent periods of years in Europe, breeding horses, playing polo with the aristocracy, with an open account at every branch of Cartier, crossing America and Europe in hired trains, seducing famous women, from Italian countesses to opera divas. In exchange, they got all kinds of pleasure and never complained about their investments – because, for them, that was what the money was for. No rich Brazilian knew how to live as well as the Guinles.

But the extravagance also had its generous side. At the very least, they disseminated beauty: their properties in Rio, Petrópolis, Teresópolis, and even on Brocoió island in Guanabara bay, were architectural jewels. Some are still standing: one of their palaces, in Laranjeiras, became the residence of the President of the Republic (today the Governor of the state of Rio lives there); others became foreign embassies. On the way, they performed many services. It was a Guinle who took the black flautist Pixinguinha and several other Brazilian musicians, classical and popular, to play in Europe in the twenties. Another helped Fluminense, the family's favourite club, by building its football stadium and its magnificent headquarters in Laranjeiras, on land he himself donated. Still another founded a hospital, the Gaffrée-Guinle, which was free to the poor. Even the Copacabana Palace was a kind of philanthropic gift to the rich: with 230 rooms and an average of three employees for *each guest*, it was born losing money. It had to be – not even daily caravans of caliphs and rajahs would have been able to support that kind of luxury.

Octavio Guinle, the son of the patriarch, built the Copa in the old style: with love – and lots of money. The cement came from Germany; the marble, from Carrara; the bronzes, from Venice; the chandeliers, from Czechoslovakia; the porcelain, from Limoges; the furniture, from Sweden; the chef Auguste Escoffier, from the Savoy hotel in London; and everything else, the glass, cutlery, uniforms, accent and the star of the inaugural ball, Mistinguett, came from France. The guests came from those parts too, because, as soon as it was opened, the Copa became part of the international circuit. In 1933, when Hollywood reconstructed it in a studio for *Flying Down to Rio*, with Fred and Ginger (it was the couple's first movie together, and they dance 'The Carioca'), the Copa had already lived with all kinds of royalty for ten years: the real ones with crowns, those with talent and creativity, those with nothing but loads of cash to their name, and powerful people in general.

It was in one of its rooms, in 1929, that President Washington Luiz was shot and wounded by his mistress, Yvonette Martin – but the scandal was kept within the hotel itself, and the bullet wound was turned into an 'operation for appendicitis'. It was also in the Copa, in 1931, that the future King Edward VIII had a romance with the carioca socialite Negra Bernardez, and, back in London, bombarded her with letters asking her to move there. It was from the window of his room in the Copa, in 1942, that Orson Welles flung chairs into the pool, furious at being dumped by phone by his lover, the Mexican star Dolores del Rio; in a rare gesture, the hotel forgave him. And it was when she was starring in the Golden Room, the venue for the Copa's big shows, that Marlene Dietrich, in 1959 – thirty years after *The Blue Angel* – asked for an ice-bucket full of sand to be put behind the curtains, so that she could have a discreet pee between 'Lili

Marlene' and 'Falling in Love Again', without needing to go to her dressing room (her dress was so tight she couldn't lift it up to her waist). These and other stories are part of the saga of the Copacabana Palace and are well known. What you wonder is: what about the stories that were never told, involving people so important that Rio never even found out they were here because the hotel, behaving impeccably as always, never let the news get out? Through its reception rooms, restaurants and bedrooms, there moved many people like that. And, as was second nature to Octavio Guinle, the hotel never let a guest go to its head.

There was no reason for the ship to budge. But, just because it existed, the sand around it was transformed.

Copacabana was the first neighbourhood in Brazil to be born cosmopolitan. There's no memory of a rural, suburban or provincial past – of the sedimentary process that makes most cities. There was no time for that. In fact, it was as if there was no 'past': nothing meaningful happened there in colonial or imperial times. Copacabana was born with the Republic. When it opened its eyes, it was already the twentieth century. But surprisingly, its pioneers already felt their roots had been planted in the sand. Along with the first Norman-style bungalows, inhabited by the rich and by foreigners, came the services that make a real city: electricity, gas, phones, transport, planned streets, shops, its own newspaper (the weekly *Beira-Mar* [Seaside]), and even a cabaret, the Mère Louise, which rented rooms by the hour and had the glory of being the precursor of 'sinfulness' in a place where the word would never have much meaning. Alongside the Copa in 1923, the first apartment blocks went up, some as luxurious as the hotel itself, and whose inhabitants led the lives of characters out of Edith Wharton. With them came cinemas, restaurants, bars and more hotels. From 1930 onwards, the bungalows were replaced by 'skyscrapers' (the sky was lower in those days) – buildings ninety feet high, one lined up right against another, forming a wall of whiteness. Then arrived the middle class, the banks, schools, hospitals, doctors' surgeries, travel agencies, casinos and all kinds of shops. In 1940, as the ads proclaimed, you could be born, live and die in Copacabana without having to leave it. But who wanted to leave anyway?

It was the first carioca community to be born near the beach, and to make daily use of it; the first to make sport a routine and have a skin colour that distinguished it from the rest of the city; and the first to adopt, as a recipe for living, dressing less and enjoying yourself much more. In 1920, Copacabana had 17,000 inhabitants; in 1940, 74,000; in 1950, 130,000; in 1960, 183,000. Where did all these people come from? From everywhere, inside and out of Brazil, and from every social class. But their origins were left behind as soon as they went through the tunnel on the Avenida Princesa Isabel, and in a short time they adapted to the area's rhythm of life. This included intellectuals, artists, bankers, diplomats, businessmen, and also the poor, many from the north-east of Brazil, who came to work as porters, hung a cage with a bird in it on the tree opposite the building they worked in, and in the twinkling of an eye, felt as if they belonged to Copacabana. Rio was always a synthesis, not an agglomeration, and Copacabana was the summary of the synthesis.

A *samba-canção* of 1946, 'Copacabana', by João de Barro and Alberto Ribeiro, called it the '*princesinha do mar*' ['little princess of the sea']. OK – but in that case, who was the queen? In the forties and fifties, Copacabana had no competition. Compared with the Avenida Atlântica, even the Promenade des Anglais in Nice and the Croisette in Cannes which had inspired it, paled into insignificance. Neither of these two avenues had its length and the beauty of its curve – not to speak of other curves. And life in those two delightful resorts in the South of France was always limited to the *saison*, while in Copacabana it went on all year round – its fixed, everyday population was the equivalent of that of Nice at the height of the European season. But it wasn't just that. If Copacabana was Nice and Cannes rolled into one, it also had its Marseilles side – less legal, less respectable, with gigolos, smugglers, kept women and suspect men behind their respectable façades. And, in the thirteen years when gambling was legal in Brazil, from 1933 on, Copacabana was

Monte Carlo as well; its two casinos, the Atlântico and the Copa (as well as the most famous, in Urca close by), swallowed fortunes and brought rivers of cash into the area. With so much money, the casinos could afford to bring whatever attractions they wanted, and so it was that during the war Bing Crosby, then bigger than Sinatra, came to Rio. The French came *en masse*: Maurice Chevalier, Jean Sablon, Charles Trenet, Edith Piaf, Yves Montand. Some came to stay, like Ray Ventura's orchestra, with Paul Misraki as its arranger and Henri Salvador as a crooner – they spent years in the Urca casino and only left after the war, duly impregnated with samba.

In 1946, a moralistic government shut Brazil's casinos (and put tens of thousands of people who depended on them out of a job). The ones who played for big stakes, Brazilians among them, cashed in their chips and went to play in Las Vegas, which still only had rattlesnakes and a hotel in the desert, the Flamingo, owned by the gangster Bugsy Siegel. And that was that. Inevitably, Las Vegas became Las Vegas, and when his mandate was finished the moralistic President, the old Marshal Dutra, went home, put his pyjamas on and went to sleep.

It would have taken more than that to kill Copacabana. On the contrary, the closing of the casinos caused a flowering of the nightclubs, more or less as had happened in New York with the end of Prohibition and the speakeasies. Hardly had the roulette-wheels stopped spinning, than Copacabana started a real industry of the wee hours, with its clubs open from seven at night to seven in the morning. Dozens of them, more or less luxurious, as you moved from the Leme to Lido square, then from the Beco das Garrafas [Bottle Alley] to the Copacabana Palace and, after a residential 'hiatus', reappearing and occupying Postos 5 and 6 – close to each other, the clubs were along the beach as well as in the streets inside the built-up area itself, in the cul-de-sacs, in the hotels and anywhere there was room for ten tables and a piano. Some became legends, like the Vogue, the Sacha, the Plaza, the Drink, the Arpège, the Meia-Noite [Midnight], the Clube da Chave [Key Club], and later, the Cangaceiro [Bandit] and Fred's. These were the biggest and most expensive, and, with the quantity of politicians, film stars, and celebrities who went there, their maîtres d'hôtel and waiters had more international experience than many ambassadors.

In the nightclubs, with their smoky atmosphere and the strong whiff of oak casks, real life was suspended. Time wasn't measured by clocks, but by the minuet of passions, flirting, sudden attraction, seduction, cheating, drunken sprees, jealousy, fights. An illicit kiss on the way to the toilet, if it was seen, could mean the end of a marriage. Not that people were puritan – far from it. The codes of behaviour in the forties and fifties really were different (though there were cases of ex-husbands and ex-wives sitting at the same table, having a whisky with their new spouses). The leading players in these nights were experienced men and women, seasoned and seductive, and no one knew what time they went to bed. Some, when they came out of the club, faced the morning sun with bags under their eyes worthy of Tristan Tzara and Theda Bara; then they went to rest their precious bodies at the Country Club.

There were also those who reconciled high jinks and practical existence, like the rich businessman Cesar Thedim, a classic example of a Rio bohemian life. The working day at his sodium sulphate factory began at six in the morning, and he was the first person there. At two in the afternoon, he felt it was enough, and went home to sleep. At eight in the evening, he awoke and went to have his day of pleasure at the Vogue, on the Avenida Princesa Isabel. There, in the early morning, he had his 'breakfast', 'lunched', danced, drank with all the most desirable women in the city and seduced some. From the club, Thedim went straight to the factory and repeated the cycle. He wasn't the only one to do this. The Vogue had the advantage of being in a hotel, where there was always a room free for amorous emergencies. The club and the hotel were destroyed in a terrible fire in 1955, but Copacabana was still crammed with temples to music and love nests.

Until 1960, whatever was publishable about this odyssey was narrated daily by the columnists specialising in nightlife. Each paper had its own, and the most influential, Antonio Maria of *Última Hora*, was himself one of the actors in this theatre of the passions. (Some day, someone will have to write the *unpublishable* story of the nightclub odyssey – who had affairs with whom, the revenges that were taken, the fortunes and the women that changed hands.) Nobody seemed to be surprised that this nocturnal extravaganza took place in an area universally known for its sun.

And there was the music, the vast backdrop for Copacabana's *dolce vita*. All the nightclubs had live music, as did many bars and restaurants; it wasn't unusual for the music to go out into the streets, when singers and musicians would visit each other during intervals in the shows and meet in the bars near the clubs. There were orchestras, small groups, piano trios with guitar and double bass, vocal groups, solo pianists, great singers and others who aspired to greatness. In the light of what they would become in the future, it is striking to note that, at a certain moment in, let's say, 1955, the young Tom Jobim, Newton Mendonça, João Gilberto, Luiz Bonfá, João Donato, Johnny Alf, Luiz Eça, Tito Madi, Dolores Duran, Sylvinha Telles, Sergio Ricardo, Ed Lincoln, Baden Powell, Milton Banana etc., could be working in one nightclub or another in Copacabana *on the same night*. More striking still: not many of them were the principal attraction (Tito and Dolores, maybe) and none of them were famous enough to fill the house. As you may know, at the end of the decade it would be them who would create the bossa nova. But at that time, the great attractions of the Copacabana night were the organist Djalma Ferreira; the pianists Bené Nunes, Waldir Calmon and Sacha; the mouth-organist Edu; the saxophonists Moacir Silva and Cipó; singers like Dorival Caymmi, Ivon Curi, Carmélia Alves, Elizeth Cardoso, Nora Ney, Dick Farney, Lucio Alves, and Murilinho de Almeida, now forgotten, who was a Cole Porter specialist.

Rio was always musically cosmopolitan, and in the Copacabana nightclubs you could hear all the available rhythms of the post-war period: foxtrots, boogie-woogies, French *chansons*, boleros, mambos, rumbas, calypsos, tangos, Portuguese fados, even flamencos and tarantellas – often filtered through the samba, with its enormous flexibility for absorbing any rhythm and going on being samba. The Orquestra Tabajara, led by the clarinettist Severino Araújo, was influenced by Artie Shaw; there were echoes of Benny Goodman in the band led by Zaccarias, another clarinettist. With the same training as the big bands, they tried fusing swing, then the leading genre, and other rhythms then in fashion, one of them being the *baião* – with better results than the American orchestras who tried to play Latin rhythms in the States. Bongos, maracas, solovoxes and other instruments foreign to Brazilian music were incorporated into the samba and, except for a purist here or there, nobody got hot under the collar. It was the beginning of the end of nationalism in music. Little by little, the nightclubs began to exercise a decisive influence on Brazilian music, making it softer and more intimate, making the melody more sophisticated, lowering the singers' tone, simplifying the rhythmic accompaniment. Because of everything that happened musically in the clubs during the fifties, we can say that, when it happened, around 1958, bossa nova was simply inevitable.

Because it was a creation of the twentieth century, sometimes thought of as the 'American century', it was natural that Copacabana should have been a pioneer in some of the United States' more dubious contributions to humanity: Coca-Cola, bubblegum, jeans, kitchenettes, rock 'n' roll. It was also the first place in Brazil where people had the privilege of smearing themselves with ketchup dripping from a hamburger swallowed in a hurry at the plastic counter of a snack bar. In spite of this, somehow Copacabana has managed to preserve a 'European' identity, more in tune with the city of Rio itself.

This identity was still in the art deco façades and doorways, in the elegance of the restaurants and hotels, in the little markets and greengrocers that survive, in the romantic steep, narrow streets and steps that can be found off the main side roads, in the hundred-year-old fishermen's colony in Posto 6 – and it's still there today. It's one of the areas of Rio least infected with the plague of shopping malls – there's only one and, even then, it's almost on the border with Ipanema. Copacabana is European too in the private collections of its oldest inhabitants: there are apartments crammed with pictures, furniture, *objets d'art*, books and documents whose only drawback is that they aren't open to the public. Sometimes one of these people dies and their collection, instead of being sent to a museum or a foundation, is cannibalised by the family and goes to enrich auctioneers, antique dealers and second-hand bookshops. For me, however, greater than the loss of the bric-a-brac is the loss of the person himself. A part of the city's memory is buried with him, someone with civilised habits and a sensibility formed in an active life. I know this because when I've cornered one of their books second-hand – especially if it's an old book about Rio – I see their annotations in ink in the margins, the observations they've added, their personal information. The royal-blue ink the comments are made in might have faded, but you can still hear the conversation between the reader and the book.

But, above all, Copacabana always was and still is 'European' in its behaviour: free of the restrictions the police have tried to impose from time to time, and which have always ended in failure. Only there could there have been a dispute between the Vice-President of the Republic and a footballer over the curvaceous Angelita Martinez, a star of the vaudeville stage (the footballer won) – and only there would the star's neighbours not give a toss about it, even when the politician, in his urge to re-establish the status quo, tried to shoot the lock on his ex-lover's door to bits. We might just mention that the player was Garrincha. The columnist Antonio Maria decided to calculate, one night, the number of love affairs, adulterous or not, that were happening in one Copacabana block, basing himself on the number of lit or half-lit windows he could see from the street. There were lots – he gave up.

And perhaps no neighbourhood in a Latin city, except in Rome under Hadrian, has been as indifferent to gay people. In Rio, from the sixties on, the Galeria Alaska, a small area of Posto 6, already worked informally as a homosexual hang-out, free from troubles and pressures and only subject to a few jokes. This is not to be sniffed at, for in Paris at that time, those who went to gay bars and night-clubs still had the police breathing down their necks. It was something like this *laissez-faire* attitude that the American poet Elizabeth Bishop found when she moved to Rio in 1951, and, guided by Lota de Macedo Soares, found her way into the lesbian-chic circle in Rio – yes, it did exist, discreet but active. Lota herself, a self-taught architect who lived in Leme, was better known for her intelligence and professional ability – we owe her the design of Flamengo park – than for her long 'marriage' to Bishop.

Copacabana didn't waste time rooting around in the lives of its inhabitants, but there was always someone to point an accusing finger. If Rio's visibility *vis-à-vis* the rest of Brazil inflates everything that happens, for a long time this visibility was concentrated on Copacabana. For outsiders, it was the neighbourhood of 'sin'. Its women were 'fallen'; its men, amoral; its young people were delinquents. This was the initial point of view of people who, when they got to Copacabana, instantly felt themselves to be yokels. But this 'doomed' state became a stigma, and so contributed to the fact that, of the three most sensational crimes in Rio in the fifties, two happened there: the attempt on the life of the journalist Carlos Lacerda in front of his apartment block on the Rua Tonelero in August 1954 (which resulted in the suicide of the President, Getúlio Vargas, three weeks later), and the death of the student Aida Curi, raped by two young men and thrown from a penthouse flat on the Avenida Atlântica in 1958. It wasn't *de rigueur* for these scandals to take place in Copacabana. But the truth is that, even with all the lights on (the ones along the beach were already the famous 'pearl necklace' in 1922), the Copacabana night always had something of the atmosphere of a French B-movie about it – *Bob le Flambeur* (1955) by Jean-Pierre Melville and *À Bout de Souffle* (1959), by Jean-Luc Godard, could have been filmed in its streets.

The B-side won out in the end. Copacabana was the victim of its own charm. All humanity dreamed of moving there some day, and half actually did. Only twenty years after it was built, the Copacabana Palace (remember it?) could only be distinguished from its neighbours by its class and beauty, no longer by its size. In photos taken in the fifties, depending on the angle, you could hardly make it out in the jungle of buildings that had taken over. Some of these buildings consisted of one-room apartments – the bedroom and sitting room were combined – with dozens of apartments on every floor and a horde of tenants and hangers-on in every one. In 1963 this type of construction was forbidden, but only after the horse had bolted – at that time, the number of people in Copacabana already led some people to ask in alarm what would happen if all the people living there decided to come out on to the street at the same time. And then, the greatest enemy of the big cities came on to the scene *en masse*: the car. The number of cars in Copacabana was frightening. The Avenida Atlântica was doubled in width, pushing the sea far away from the apartment windows, but not even that resolved the problem.

In 1980, Copacabana had almost 230,000 inhabitants – more than the population of many medium-sized European cities. It had all the plagues resulting from this inordinate growth: services got worse, living conditions deteriorated, dirt increased, the luxury shops moved, the tourists stayed away. Adult nightlife, with well-cut jackets and heaving bosoms, had long ago moved to Ipanema – in its place, there was a blasé bohemian crowd, drinking on the cheap, unshaven and with knapsacks on their backs. When Copacabana had its hundredth birthday in 1992, all the reports lamented its terrible decline. A word was coined in Rio to designate wonderful neighbourhoods that allowed themselves to be destroyed by voracious property development to which the authorities turned a blind eye: Copacabanisation. It's an ungrateful expression for the neighbourhood to which Brazil owes the real beginning of its modernisation.

But even then, without us realising it, some things were beginning to happen. In 1989, the Guinles, whose fortune had dissolved in their luxurious lifestyle, sold the last jewel in the crown, the Copa, to an Anglo-American businessman, James Sherwood, who had just picked up another legendary hotel, the Cipriani in Venice. Sherwood took years restoring the Copa to its original glory and modernising it without affecting its major characteristics – the work cost him double the twenty-three million dollars he'd paid for the hotel. At the same time, new five-star hotels arose along the beach, and the traditional hotels, like the Lancaster (where Cary Grant and Ingrid Bergman 'stayed' in *Notorious*), the Excelsior and the Ouro Verde, were updated. The beach was newly lit. Attracted by the new year celebrations and by Carnival, the tourists began to come back, and not just to buy stuffed piranhas and trays lined with butterfly wings. This could only mean one thing: Copacabana was a good bet again.

The bet began to pay off in the nineties, and some of the results can be seen today. For nine months of the year, the beach is no longer deserted at night. The kiosks are crowded, couples walk along the promenade, football is played on the sand till dawn. The bars along the beach have cleaned up their act, the old restaurants have got their clientele back and new ones have joined them. A specialised but attractive range of shops – second-hand bookshops, Internet cafés, craft bakers, friendly bistros – are appearing little by little. Modern Sound, which was already the best record shop in Brazil, and one of the best in the world, has tripled in size and annexed a bistro where, every day, from five to nine at night, you can hear four or five different languages – they are the real language of Copacabana. It's true that, at night, prostitutes and transvestites invade certain streets and that, at any time of the day or night, it's not a good idea for a Swedish woman to walk around covered in gold and jewels. But where is that a good idea?

To general surprise, it's also been discovered that the population of Copacabana has fallen. With the surplus out of the way – they've spent the last couple of decades moving to the Barra da Tijuca – official statistics have revealed that, in 2000, it's gone down to 155,000. If these numbers are right, they bring the population of Copacabana back to 1955 levels.

The majority of the population also reminds one of 1955. Copacabana, which just yesterday seemed so young, now has the highest average age in Rio – twenty-one per cent of its inhabitants are 'old'.

Now widows and widowers live there, retired generals and civil servants. But don't expect to find them in wheelchairs, reeking of mothballs, a beret on their heads and a tartan plaid on their knees. On the contrary. Nowhere can you see so many white-haired citizens at seven in the morning, their skin tanned and their muscles showing all their knots, as strong as oxen, playing volleyball at the same beach net they used when they were young, and with the same friends. The balls may be hit less hard, but any young lad who risks challenging them may find he's in for a surprise. Many of them still play the sports that Copacabana pioneered worldwide: beach football, invented there in the 1910s, beach tennis, in the 1940s, and foot-volleyball, in the 1970s. It's not surprising these veterans should still be in good shape because, in the past, some were champions at underwater fishing, professional divers or trainers of football teams. Even their headquarters is the same as it was years ago: the Marimbás, the club at Posto 6, facing the Atlantic Ocean and the Serra do Mar. There, for decades, they have swum, fished, made love and taken part in Carnival balls from which the police, prudently, have preferred to keep a safe distance.

Oh, yes, that question: 'What would happen if the whole population of Copacabana decided to come out on to the streets at the same time?'

Well, one day, that was exactly what happened. Worse: with them came a multitude from every area of Rio, as well as domestic and foreign tourists. Even so, the dreaded catastrophe didn't happen. It was during a *réveillon* in the middle of the eighties – the first time more than a million people dressed in white had gathered on the Avenida Atlântica to throw flowers into the sea and watch the fireworks at midnight on 31 December. Since then, it's taken place every year, and with more people every time – the *réveillon* of the year 2000, the last of the millennium, was estimated at four million people.

Yemanja, the goddess of the waters, answers the 'requests' made of her in exchange for flowers. In the past, she probably found the task easier. After all, on New Year's Eve, she used only to be visited by harmless devotees of *umbanda* and *candomblé* who spontaneously lit their candles in the sand, offered her flowers and begged for this favour or that. There were already tens of thousands of people in Copacabana, but all had a profound faith in her powers. Since the festival has begun to be regulated by the authorities and has been trans-formed into an event for millions of people, I don't know if Yemanja's busy schedule can find room for so many petitions. And I doubt she can feel com-fortable in the middle of such a racket. Maybe that's why the real faithful have brought their homage forward. Now they go and throw flowers on the night of the thirtieth, which is much quieter. Others have gone to more distant beaches, far from the madding crowd. For these radical believers,

Copacabana is terminally corrupted for religious purposes.

Maria Graham's time has well and truly gone. The Copacabana *réveillon* has become an event. The spectacle of the human mass arriving little by little at the Avenida Atlântica, during the day, is already something. At five in the afternoon, there are easily a million people there. When night falls, about eight o'clock, there are two million. The sellers of kebabs, canned beer and all kinds of junk give the promenade the look of an amusement park. In the hotels and the buildings facing the sea, the rooms and apartments are lit up for the rich people's *réveillons* – the fabulous private parties, whose windows with a view of the beach are fought over and booked months before (those of the Copacabana Palace, a year before). The doorways swallow up men in summer jackets and women you wouldn't believe. The night proceeds and, there below, on the pavements, people are still arriving, ninety per cent in white, filling up the side streets and emptying out *en masse* on to the beach. A few minutes before midnight, more than three million people have already occupied every part of the avenue. The signal for the beginning of the year, coming out of the loudspeakers, is 'Cidade maravilhosa'. Suddenly, in the midst of the music, the fireworks burst into the sky.

There is a minimum of twenty minutes of fireworks over the sea, which shoot from six different points, as well as a cascade of lights that comes down a thirty-eight-storey hotel and another that sends sparks up from Copacabana fort. It's unforgettable for anyone who watches, not so much for the fireworks as for the sensation of being in the middle of so many people kissing and hugging each other, and giving good wishes for a better new year. Where do cariocas get the energy for so much partying and happiness? Nothing can guarantee that the new year really will be better, that the sea will be calmer, that prosperity will knock on their door, but, at that moment, nothing can overcome their enthusiasm. Clearing away any dark thoughts, six simultaneous mega-shows explode, with Brazilian singers, on the stages set up along the beach. It's the biggest popular festival in the world, two or three times bigger than the new year festivals in Sydney harbour, the Champs-Élysées or Times Square. The party goes on till dawn, and considering the quantity of people who are dancing and drinking, the number of stolen wallets, alcoholic blackouts, fights, and accidents is almost zero – it's the most exciting, and, paradoxically, the safest night of the year in Rio. It's also the most beautiful.

When they go unwillingly back home, the multitude leaves 300 tons of rubbish on the asphalt and the sand – rubbish which, by eight in the morning of 1 January has already been picked up by 3,000 binmen, down to the last drinking straw. The sea does the job of swallowing the flowers that have been thrown into it.

Ruy Castro

The world awakes a year older. In Rio, two lovely young girls in bikinis get to the beach early. You can hear the sound of drumming. Summer is tingling hot, and Carnival's on its way.

GLOSSARY

agogô: a musical instrument, of African origin, made of two bell-shaped pieces of metal. It is played by being hit with another piece of metal.

baião: a popular dance from the northern state of Bahia, usually accompanied by a guitar and an accordion.

batucada / batuque: an Afro-Brazilian dance, accompanied by singing and heavy percussion.

cachaça: cheap, and very strong, liquor distilled from sugar-cane juice.

caipirinha: a popular drink made with *cachaça*, crushed limes, ice and sugar.

candomblé: the most traditional of the Brazilian religions of African (Yoruba) origin.

capoeira: a martial art, based on skilled use of kicking, developed by Brazilian slaves as a means of self-defence and attack. It was much persecuted in the past, but has now become a popular sport and art form.

cateretê: a dance of rural origins, performed in parallel lines, with hand-clapping and stomping of the feet.

choro: a sentimental and intricate kind of music played by a band made up of flutes, and both full-size and small guitars, along with other instruments. Its origins are in nineteenth-century Rio.

cuíca: an instrument resembling a small drum, made to resonate by vibrating a cord inside it, which is very typical of samba.

farofa: manioc flour, fried and often mixed with eggs and bacon; a common side-dish.

feijoada: a heavy stew of black beans (*feijão*) with pieces of pork, dried beef and sausage, and served with *farofa*, shredded spring cabbage, and slices of orange. It is often the dish of the day on Saturdays in Rio restaurants.

forró: a popular dance from the north-east of Brazil, danced in pairs. The word is now used for its musical accompaniment.

ipê: the name of many Brazilian species of trees, some of the most prevalent of which are covered with yellow or purple flowers in spring.

jambo: a tree of Asian origin (*Syzygium jambos*), with red flowers and small pink pear-shaped fruit, known in English as rose apple.

lundu: a dance of African origin, popular in the eighteenth and nineteenth centuries.

macumba: a religion with origins in *candomblé*, but with indigenous and Christian elements.

maxixe: a fast and skilful dance which appeared in Rio in the 1870s, and mixed elements of the polka with African syncopated rhythm.

modinha: a romantic form of popular song, popular in the early nineteenth century.

murici: a tree of the Byrsonima genus, sometimes known in English as the Barbados cherry.

pitanga: a small, red, bittersweet fruit from a tree which grows on sandy areas by the coast.

quilombo: a settlement created by runaway slaves.

sapucaia: a tree native to the Amazon, which produces woody capsules containing thirty or forty edible nuts.

sarapatel: a highly seasoned dish made of the blood and offal of pigs and sheep.

vatapá: a fish or chicken dish, made with coconut milk, dried and fresh prawns, stale bread, and toasted and ground peanuts and cashew nuts, and seasoned with oil from the oil palm (*azeite de dendê*).

xinxim: a chicken stew similar to *vatapá*.

A NOTE ON THE AUTHOR

Ruy Castro is a writer and journalist whose books
include two classics about bossa nova, a biography
of the immortal footballer Garrincha and an
encyclopaedia of Ipanema. He has also edited a
compendium of 1,600 poisonous *bons mots* called
Bad Humour and two novels for children. His book
*Bossa Nova: The Story of the Brazilian Music that
Seduced the World* was published in the US in 2001.

A NOTE ON THE TYPE

The text of this book is set in Linotype Sabon,
named after the type founder, Jacques Sabon. It
was designed by Jan Tschichold and jointly
developed by Linotype, Monotype and Stempel, in
response to a need for a typeface to be available in
identical form for mechanical hot metal
composition and hand composition using foundry
type. Tschichold based his design for Sabon roman
on a fount engraved by Garamond, and Sabon
italic on a fount by Granjon. It was first used in
1966 and has proved an enduring modern classic.

BANGU
PEDRA BRANCA
JACAREPAGUÁ
MEI
PARQUE NACIONAL DA TIJUCA
GRA
LAGOA DA TIJUCA
ALTO DA BOA VISTA
PEDRA DA GAVEA
BARRA DA TIJUCA
SÃO CONRADO
JARDIM BOTÂNICO
GÁVEA
LAGOA
LEBLON
IPANEMA
COPAC
O C E A N O
ARPOADOR